THE POLITICS
OF
MANAGEMENT

THE POLITICS OF MANAGEMENT

Andrew Kakabadse

Gower

Published by
Gower Publishing Company Limited
Aldershot, Hants, England

British Library Cataloguing in Publication Data

Kakabadse, Andrew
   The politics of management
   1 Personnel management
   2 Interpersonal relations
   I Title
   658 3'15 HF5549

ISBN 0-566-02430-6

Printed and bound in Great Britain by
Biddles Ltd, Guildford and King's Lynn

Contents

Preface

Question – what does the manager's job involve?

Answer – the manager's job involves getting work done through other people, irrespective of whether the work is to do with finance, production, personnel, marketing, etc. The manager should know something about the particular subject area in question, but he has to know a great deal more about the people he is directing, supervising and co-ordinating to ensure that the job gets done. A manager will operate effectively only when his technical skills are matched by his people skills.

This book is about the people element of work. It is about the interactions that take place among people at work. It is about the relationships that people develop with each other whilst doing their work. It is about the complications that arise whilst conducting seemingly straightforward work relationships. These interactions, relationships and complications I call 'the politics of management'.

I argue that the politics of management are of vital importance to both the individual and his development and to the organisation and its growth and prosperity. I indicate that simply doing a good job is not enough in today's work organisations. If you are ambitious for promotion, increased status, control over your own business and/or a bigger income, or, at the other extreme, if you just simply wish to be left alone to do your job in your own quiet way, then knowing how politics develop and how to handle them is of prime consideration. I suggest that you are unlikely to be promoted, or even left alone, unless you know how to become effectively involved with others.

The book is written in a light-hearted style. Virtually all the key points made are backed by real-life case studies. For reasons of confidentiality, people's names and places have been changed, except for some certain cases where I identify the source of reference.

Do not let the somewhat simplistic, conversational style fool you. This is a serious text, conveying an important message. It is written for all those who recognise that work is one of the most influential forces that shape our individual lives.

Andrew Kakabadse

Acknowledgements

I would like to thank Chris Parker of Cranfield School of Management and John Irwin of Gower for their invaluable advice and ideas during the first stages of writing this book. In addition, many thanks to Malcolm Stern of Gower for the dexterous and effective use of his editorial pen on the penultimate script.

My gratitude also to Sue Brown and Sarah Biston for their patience, good humour and high quality work in typing draft after draft to produce this text.

Finally, a special thank you to my wife Patricia for her support and understanding over this last year, and to my one-year-old daughter Sophia who decided to sleep through the night so her father could write in the early morning.

APK

Why the Politics of Management?

The answer is simple. Politics in organisations are ever present. No matter who you are, or what you do, it is impossible to escape the power/political interactions that take place between people at work. The point was aptly made by Professor Lyman Porter of UCLA,* at one of his international lectures (1981), who reported a study he had recently conducted examining the successful and unsuccessful promotion bids by management executives. Porter discovered that those successfully promoted attributed their success to their abilities; and those whose promotion bids failed attributed their lack of success to politics – either they thought that they were out of favour or someone else was more in favour than themselves. For the unsuccessful, politics was seen as an unpleasant, negative but most powerful experience. Porter concluded that politics in organisations are probably the most important influence on a manager's development.

There can be little doubt that Porter's conclusion is accurate. Most people in organisations recognise that simply doing a good job is not sufficient. For people who are more ambitious, attaining professional competence is only the first step. To achieve high office relatively rapidly requires skills in negotiation, in forward planning, in making projects work, in getting on with people; ironically it requires skills in being different, and yet in being able to fit in with superiors, colleagues and subordinates. For others not so fortunate as to be in the forefront of the promotion stakes, their time at work may be spent vying for limited resources simply to get a good job done, competing for limited status positions or just in attracting the attention of a senior executive. It is easy to see how politics come

* University of California, Los Angeles.

1

to be identified as negative.

Now consider the situation at group level. Certain groups in organisations may wish to preserve their identity based on a professional ethos, geographic location or previous tradition; all of which may be in direct conflict with the expressed wishes of corporate management. Other groups may attempt to preserve their values and identity but have no wish to confront their superiors openly. They may seem to accept new systems of working but covertly tamper with those systems to meet their needs.

If the actions and intentions of others can be easily misinterpreted; if groups and individuals confront and oppose one another; if the skills of negotiation and manoeuvre are as important as task skills for promotion to senior management, why then are politics in organisations not given greater attention? After all, politics seem to pervade every inch of our lives. There are two main reasons.

First, writers, researchers and managers are not able to agree on the true meaning of the terms *power, politics* and *influence*. An inability to agree on basic principles, coupled with the taboo nature of the subject, has made politics an under-examined area of study.

Second, writers, researchers and managers have not quite come to terms with the fact that life in organisations has as much to do with the differences as with the similarities between people. Theorists and practitioners alike have preferred to believe that similarities bind people together, for example, believing that managers have the right to manage; that managers should be the motivators; in other words, that the most appropriate way to live our lives is to accept the principle of *downward influence*. Yet all too often, life in terms of strife and conflict has shown that downward influence is supposition rather than fact.

Whatever the experts say, political processes in organisations are an integral part of life in organisations. This statement is based on the premise that the differences, rather than the similarities between people, form the reality of life in organisations.

As a prelude to understanding politics in organisations, we must determine what sort of differences exist in them.

DIFFERENCES IN ORGANISATIONS

How do differences arise? In all organisations, individuals and groups compete for resources, for attention, for influence; there are differences of opinion as to the priorities and objectives to be attained; clashes of values and beliefs occur with common frequency. All these factors lead to the formation of pressure groups, vested interests, cabals, personal rivalries, personality clashes, hidden deals and bonds of alliance. Probably, most people spend most of their time managing conflict, competition and the formation of alliances as an everyday part of their work load. The first step to becoming effective at managing differences is to understand how they arise.

Grand strategy *v* local identity

All organisations are involved in some form of planning. The greater the perceived need for effectiveness, the greater the need to plan on a broad scale. As part of the planning process, managers may identify policies for change; new areas of investment; there may be a need to change the location of plants and offices. Equally, a recently appointed senior executive may feel it necessary to stamp his authority on the organisation, thereby introducing changes which represent his unique contribution.

Table 1.1

Grand strategy	*v*	Local conditions
Policies for change		Identity with existing group patterns
New product lines		Identity with existing work patterns
New investment		New developments of little interest to locals
New technologies		
		Certain skills no longer required
Re-training personnel		
		People identify with old skills
Closure of plants		
		Redundancy
Opening new plants		
		Transfer of personnel

Whatever the reasons for change, large-scale changes are likely to disrupt local conditions (see Table 1.1). Re-organisation of systems and enterprise structure, the introduction of new technologies or product lines and the lack or increase of investment, are at best likely to disrupt existing groupings of people and patterns of friendship, and at worst could mean moving to another area or redundancy. There is little doubt that changes at the policy level do disrupt people's lives.

As one group of people appreciates the need for change and for the future of the enterprise, another group's concern centres on the negative effects of change upon its locality. Mistrust and fundamental differences of beliefs and values develop, irrespective of how sensitively management attempts to implement its change strategy.

Gouldner's study

As early as the mid 1950's, social scientists were examining the effects of change on organisations. Gouldner's (1954) study of a gypsum plant and mine that underwent a major and dramatic change of top personnel, is a classic example. The former manager of the gypsum mine had engaged in loose, almost indulgent practices with regard to the observation rules and standards of work. Head office, in wishing to increase the production record of the plant, replaced the old manager with a new man. The new manager well understood his mandate to increase productivity and decided to ignore the pattern of indulgence established by the previous man. He enforced the existing rules and regulations. The system came to be viewed by the operatives as punishment-centred. Internal tensions and stress increased, resulting in redundancies and the hiring of new labour. Unlike his predecessor, the new manager did not become active in the community surrounding the plant and also did not generate a loyal cadre of subordinates.

Gouldner termed those who go along with grand strategy as *Cosmopolitans* and those with local conditions as *Locals*. He concluded that as with the gypsum plant case, by not taking into account the sentiments of the Locals, management's attempts at change can be disrupted, diverted or destroyed by the Locals.

Superiors *v* subordinates

The one area that has attracted substantial attention in the study of organisations has been the superior/subordinate relationship. As early as 1911, Frederick Taylor identified the superior/subordinate relationship as crucial to developing a successful and effective organisation. These writings concen-

trated on establishing the key factors in the roles people held
that would lead to an efficient and workable relationship.

Other researchers and writers have examined the superior/
subordinate relationship from the point of view of the manager
learning to collaborate with colleagues, superiors and subordinates; from the point of view of appraising individuals in
their current job in order to pick out those suitable for further
training and promotion.

Throughout, the underlying characteristic of the vast majority
of the studies on the superior/subordinate relationship has been
to focus on finding ways in which the relationship can be made
to work better, irrespective of whether the emphasis was on role
or individual motivation.

No wonder such attention has been given, for, in practice, the
superior/subordinate relationship has led to wide differences
developing between people (see Table 1.2).

Table 1.2

Superior	v	Subordinate
May or may not be given adequate authority in role to manage		May or may not respect that authority
Belief in the right to manage		May or may not respect the individual manager
Increased salary and status		Conscious of salary and status differences
Try to motivate subordinates		Subordinates may see attempts to motivate as manipulation

The reason that differences emerge between people in the
organisation hierarchy could be twofold. First, role reasons: the
manager may not be given sufficient authority to carry out the
duties required of him. Second, personal reasons: the manager
may not be sufficiently skilled to establish a positive and
comfortable working relationship with his subordinates. The
subordinate, for example, may be obstructive towards the
superior due to the superior's lack of social, technical or
planning and administrative skills. It becomes that much more
difficult to stimulate a genuinely effective working relationship
when, from the subordinate's view, someone of lower ability but

higher salary has the right to direct other people as he desires. People may eventually oppose and undermine the individual manager and further offer little commitment to the organisation.

Although managers may be appointed to pull people together and develop effective teams, the superior/subordinate relationship can generate more differences than similarities.

Management *v* operatives

In the superior/subordinate relationship, both parties are likely to share the same sense of identity with organisations and pursue the same rewards – promotion, status, recognition. Differences are likely to arise out of dislike or disrespect.

In contrast, conflicts between management and the shop floor are due to basic differences of belief as to how people should conduct themselves at work and at home.

Consider how differences of beliefs, values and norms arise

Table 1.3

Manager	*v*	Operative
Myth of owner		Reality of shop floor employee
Works on longer-term time span		Works to short-term objectives
Allocates resources		Responds to management's allocation
Hires/fires		Maintains a steady job
Promoted upwards		Negotiates for increased pay
Individualistic work style		Accepts work group norms
Salary		Wages
Suit as the working garment		Overalls as the working garment
Various social interests		Local community interests

(Table 1.3). Although both groups fall under the category of employees, managers tend to conform to the myth of acting as the owner. Understandably so, for the decisions a manager makes and his style of operation would be identical to those of any owner.

Hence, for any manager to operate effectively, it is important for him to share the norms and values of his employing organisation and feel that he has a reasonable chance of substantial reward for his endeavours. That is not the case with the work force operatives. Due to the nature of the tasks they are asked to perform, they can produce work to a reasonable standard and not necessarily share in part or whole the ethos of their employing organisation.

The tasks of the manager will involve planning, product and market development; tasks that require a long-term timespan. Operatives' tasks require the completion of reasonably well specified sub-tasks to a required standard; the attitude an individual develops towards his work under such circumstances is short-term – finish the job.

In preparing for the future, the manager will need to consider the way resources (including people) are allocated and who to hire for a job in order to achieve optimum results. Shop floor operatives must respond to the manager's direction.

Whereas a manager stands or falls according to his own performance, work force operatives subscribe to a group culture, partly as a defence against management and partly in an attempt to stimulate satisfactory working relationships.

Even socially, wide-ranging differences arise. In terms of dress, individuals in both groups will have accumulated a different wardrobe for work. Managers wear the higher status suit, operatives the lower status overall or casual dress such as jeans and tee-shirts.

Where groups of people think, feel and conduct their work and social life so differently to one another, stereotyped beliefs develop. From the manager's point of view, such beliefs could be *the manager's right to manage and the manager's right to control*. From the shop floor operatives' viewpoint, a widespread belief may be that *management is uncaring or irresponsive to employee needs*. Although stereotyped, people do conduct their work lives according to such values.

Professional *v* administrator

The values we have looked at so far have been determined by the hierarchy or the shop floor. The additional strong determinant of beliefs in organisations is the profession.

The professional will place marked emphasis on the quality of work he produces. He may see each new task as a challenge to his professional expertise. The task may have to be tackled in a slightly different way to all other previous tasks. Consequently the professional, whether engineer, doctor, lawyer, teacher or social worker, would probably attempt to tackle each job as he saw fit and not refer to the organisation for guidance.

In contrast, the administrator would not hold such allegiances. His work performance and career aspirations would be directed by the demands of the organisation. The classic image of the administrator, if not entirely accurate, is of a person who only identifies with his employing organisation – do no more or less than what is required of you; preserve the hierarchy; actions should be determined by your role requirements – all of which are the antithesis of the values of professional practice (see Table 1.4).

Table 1.4

Professional	*v*	Administrator
Emphasis on professional quality of work		Doing no more or less than what is required
Actions determined by the professional ethos		Actions determined by role requirements
Often a strong team identity		Preserve the hierarchy
Low identity with any one organisation		Career development seen as promotion up the hierarchy

Not conforming to organisational norms can lead to a lack of trust between the line manager and the specialist, especially in each other's ability to manage work problems. With the growth of specialisation, line managers should be able to delegate certain tasks to specialists. For delegation to take place, line management must have sufficient confidence in the ability of the specialists and vice versa. Such trust, however, may be difficult to generate. Where the professional has little influence over his employing organisation, he is at a distinct disadvantage for he is just one more resource to be developed or discarded according to the current objectives of the organisation. Certainly, professionals in R and D units and training personnel have traditionally been more vulnerable. During times of stringency, training and R and D are among the first to have their budgets reduced, irrespective of how well or badly they have accomplished their tasks in the past. Such conditions do little to endear the professionals to the organisation.

It is unlikely that we will ever escape the classic professional/ bureaucratic conflict.

Planning *v* execution

The theme of the professional *v* the administrator is continued (see Table 1.5). The specialist will design a particular product. The line manager will attempt the manufacture of the product according to the limitations of his budget.

Table 1.5

Planning	*v*	Execution
Professional specialist		Line manager
Market-oriented		Product-oriented
Control of expenditure		High capital outlay
Future long-term policies		Acting on present contingencies
Meeting future market needs		Restrictive work practice

The processes of product design and manufacture may not be well aligned. Much will depend on the clarity of the detailed plan of the product. Much will also depend on the personal relationship between the designer and manufacturer. How will problems that arise on the spot be handled? Will one or both groups try to make the other the scapegoat, or have they developed a sufficiently strong relationship to be able to solve the problem together?

Much the same considerations apply to the relationships between those who are market-oriented and those who are product-oriented. Marketing departments, as part of a product development campaign, may take advance orders and promise deadlines on certain goods. Production departments may be unwilling, or, more likely, unable to fulfill the marketing department's promises to clients. The result is that disagreements, loss of face and poor relationships between units in the organisation can easily develop. Such negative interactions can, after a time, become part of the tradition or culture of the organisation, which makes improving relationships an almost impossible task. It is so easy for quite serious divergences to occur between what is supposed to happen and what actually happens. Finally, both organisation and client suffer.

CRISIS OR INAPPROPRIATE THEORY?

With such differences between people who need to work together simply to achieve outputs, are we in a permanent state of crisis? Is it merely a dream that we can live, work and share problems and personal experiences with each other?

The answer is partly yes and partly no. Differences do indeed exist; yes, people think, feel and see the same situation in different ways. However, that does not have to be of overriding importance. The problem is that managers have been fed with inappropriate theory.

Consider certain basic values which many managers hold:

1 managers have the right to manage;
2 it is a manager's job to motivate his people;
3 it is a manager's responsibility to get others to work to common objectives;
4 the backbone of any company is its good middle managers.

The common theme underlying the above values is that of *shared meaning*: it is assumed that people share similar norms, attitudes, values, views of the world, feelings about situations; and that people in the same situation will share a common experience and viewpoint. Unfortunately for management theorists, people do not behave in such a predetermined manner; individuals do not pursue the same objectives; stability and equilibrium are not necessarily the norm. In fact, there is as much *unshared meaning* as *shared meaning* in organisations. There are as many differences between middle and senior management as between management and work force operatives.

A shop steward may not recognise that managers have the right to manage. In complete contrast, a shop floor operative may prefer managers to manage as his own concern is to maintain a steady and secure income. A middle manager may think managers have the right to manage, but consider his boss as incapable. He may try to undermine and usurp his boss's position and yet still believe in the structure of the hierarchy.

People in employment are led to believe in shared meaning and no more so than in management training. For managers who attend structured, semi-structured or unstructured management training programmes, strong pressures are brought to bear on each person in these terms: get involved, take part, make a contribution, work with your study group. The ultimate aim is to achieve *best fit*, i.e. you come to terms with the environment and the people around you.

Let us not swing to the other extreme. Notions of shared meaning are valuable. The 'pulling together' philosophy, especially in recession, is vital. But so often, shared meaning becomes compulsive. What happens to the idiosyncratic and creative person? History shows that creativity stems from the unusual person, the mutant gene, the persistent lone voice.

Living and interacting with other people has as much to do with unshared meaning as it has to do with shared meaning.

Understanding politics in organisations involves analysing how people manage both shared and unshared meaning.

THINKING POLITICS

Politics in organisations are about being able to reconcile the following factors: the individual and his motivation (the needs of the person), the group he deals with and its norms and behaviour, (the shared attitudes of people), the general situation in which the individual finds himself and the acceptable and unacceptable ways people interact with each other. To achieve such a reconciliation, the book is split into three parts.

Part I concentrates on why people behave the way they do; it constitutes an analysis of individual drives. A model of human behaviour and motivation is offered which studies four stereotyped organisational politicians. The patterns of action and interaction adopted by each of the four characters are discussed. It will soon become obvious to the reader that attempting to motivate people is just as 'political' as attempting to manipulate them. It all depends on *how* certain interactions are conducted, *why* they were undertaken in the first place and *what* are the views and feelings of the receiving parties once they have experienced these interactions.

In Part II, the forces or pressures that have shaped our organisations are examined. From this it emerges that certain types of organisational politicians are better suited to the situation and hence their services have been more in demand. However, the question is put, will this continue? Changes are rapidly taking place in terms of technological advancement, market demands and energy consumption. Will our organisations of the future be similar to those of today? Hence, will we need a different type of organisational politician to lead us into the future?

Whatever the answers to these questions, Part III puts forward strategies for action (to be adopted by anyone – from secretaries to company presidents). One assumption is made: our organisations are and will be facing rapid changes. Hence, in order to cope with change, or in order actually to alter the status quo, political strategies for change are discussed. The strategies relate to acting politically with individuals as well as with whole organisations. Whereas Part I is about understanding the process of politics, Part III is about acquiring power through being political. Power is seen as nothing more than knowing how to behave as an effective politician. You, as a person, need not have status, position or money to become powerful. You simply have to use your already existing skills of influence in a slightly different way from hitherto. What is more, power should not be seen in a negative light. Power is about getting things done, in your way. It is *what* you want done and *how* you want it done, that counts. Practise it right and not only you, but others around you, benefit from your presence.

The learning point in this book is that politics, as a process, are never-ending. People do think, feel and act differently to each other despite what they say. It is also necessary to be aware that the interactions between individuals and groups will strongly influence the view each individual has of himself, the contribution he makes, the rewards he receives and whether he stays or leaves his present organisation. Eventually, the pattern of politics played in any organisation could determine the success or failure of that organisation.

Part One
INDIVIDUAL
DRIVES

Appointing Frederikson (Part 1)

Chairman (smiling benevolently, hands clasped and sitting behind the long table): Well, Mr Frederikson, after having assessed all the candidates, my colleagues and I would like to offer you the job. You're just our type of man!

Frederikson: Thank you, sir. I would like to accept your offer.

Chairman (rising): Excellent. Come and join us. What do you drink?

1st senior manager (on the interviewing panel): Do you really think you can pull off the KY contract?

2nd senior manager: Yeh, if you get the KY contract, we really look forward to working with you.

Frederikson (thinks): Jesus, these people are just unreal! Can't they do things for themselves? Even if I get the KY contract, these guys couldn't handle it. First job for me is to get rid of them! Then build up my own team.

Moral

People do things for their own reasons, not yours.

1 The Four Organisational Politicians

To understand the processes of politics, it is necessary to understand the people who play politics. To understand people, I examine the contribution made by psychologists in determining personality.

DETERMINING PERSONALITY

A number of well-known psychologists and philosophers have come to similar conclusions as to why people develop particular personalities. They concluded:

1. By using their experiences from the past, people learn how to cope with the world around them.
2. Although this learning process is never ending, people, quite naturally, reject the more unsuccessful ways of coping.
3. After a while, people develop a repertoire of thoughts, feelings, behaviours and skills which is their best way of coping with their world.
4. The more successful the repertoire, the more fixed it becomes, the more people develop and form their personality.

The behavioural scientist, Irving Goffman (1974), called this repertoire *frames of reference,* a now commonly used phrase to indicate how an individual subjectively interprets the world around him. Other writers on psychology and philosophy suggest that we all structure our experiences to form a map (like a geographical map) which shows boundaries, hills, mountains, valleys, difficult routes and easy routes to follow. Just as we would use a geographical map to find the easiest or most difficult routes to follow, so we use a *mental map* to drive our behaviour. How then are mental maps and the politics of management related? The hypothesis offered is that politics constitute an influence process which can be perceived as positive or negative, depending on whether one's own mental map is being supported or threatened.

Let us explore further this notion of a mental map being supported or threatened. In my capacity as an academic consultant, many managers have said to me:

> I get on fine with my subordinates. It is just that my boss keeps on interfering with everything I do. I am getting sick of him.

In many people's minds, there seems to be a split between legitimate and illegitimate attempts at influence. In dealing downwards with subordinates, the manager feels comfortable. Managers seem to influence downwards on the basis of their knowledge of particular individuals and groups. A good manager is one whose subordinates state: 'My boss knows how to handle me!' The good manager is someone who helps subordinates feel comfortable.

Yet, in managing upwards, so many middle managers seem to use a different approach. They are so used to leading downwards that they forget that relations upwards are also a mutual dependence process. So many managers seem to stereotype people in a top–down way so that their mental map is not sufficiently flexible to cope with upward influence. They forget that bosses are people. The boss is no longer a person but a stereotype in the person's mind. Should the boss do something to break the stereotype, then the individual believes that politics are being played. Note that under such circumstances, politics are linked with negative influence.

Stereotypes of people will sooner or later be broken. Hence, is there any way of giving people insights into the width and breadth of their mental map and the mental map of others to help them understand why people do things the way they do?

I believe there is. From my observation of people, as an academic and a consultant, I can identify two fundamental drives which lead to the formation of mental maps – people's perceptions and their actions.

THE PERCEPTION/ACTION MODEL

Figure 1.1 represents the perception/action model. The model shows the dominant values people hold, the attitudes they adopt and finally, in Figure 1.2, the styles they use to put their values and attitudes into practice.

Perceptions

In Figure 1.1, the horizontal axis represents the determinants of people's perceptions, i.e. their values or beliefs, probably the most powerful factors in personality.

The two extreme ends of the continuum are *inner-directedness* and *outer-directedness*. People who are inner-directed develop their perceptions and views with little reference to the outside world. Those who are outer-directed feel a need to comply with the perceived attitudes and behaviour that others seem to exhibit in that situation.

Complying with the perceived norms of the situation is termed shared meaning. People who need to operate under conditions of shared meaning adhere to the values of the

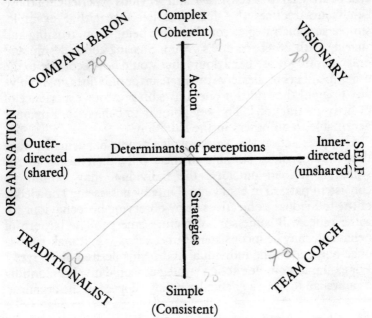

Figure 1.1   Perception/action model

organisation, the structure in the organisation, the power dependencies in the system and the monetary and status rewards the organisation offers.

People who generate their own values of life and norms of behaviour are self-dependent. They live with unshared meaning. They appreciate that a number of the people with whom they will interact feel differently to themselves, but see no need to adapt their particular views to suit others.

Actions

The vertical axis represents people's abilities to put into practice their views and values, i.e. their repertoire of action strategies. There are two alternative types of action strategies: simple and complex.

Those who practise strategies classed as simple, aim for consistency. Irrespective of whether the people in the situation work on shared or unshared meaning, the behaviours they feel they should adopt are predictable, commonly recognised and probably previously practised. In this way, individuals and groups are seen to be *consistent* and previous experience of those behaviours reduces the degree of felt threat. For example, simple action strategies could involve being open, trusting and sharing with others in one's group. Sharing comradeship and only adopting those behaviours that would be acceptable to the other members of the department, team or unit does not involve any original thought, for one draws on previous experience of positive interactions. The key point is to behave in a manner acceptable to all others in the situation.

Complex action strategies involve people behaving in ways that they consider suitable to meet only their needs in the situation. To an outsider, the individual may exhibit no consistent pattern of behaviour. Only by possessing knowledge of the individual's objectives or by observing his behaviour for some time, will some sort of picture emerge. The pattern of behaviour may be inconsistent but *coherent*, i.e. it makes sense once one knows the individual and/or his desired objectives.* For example, complex action strategies would involve planning a campaign to have a particular policy adopted in the organisa-

---

* See Chapters 6 and 7, which discuss the more complex political action strategies.

tion, identifying key people who would support the policy, influencing others who are less committed and isolating those who are against one's own ideas. Complex action strategies do involve new and original ideas and actions and possibly taking risks.

The combination of the inner/outer-directed axis and the simple/complex action strategies axis forms the individual's mental map. It is inevitable that people will interact with others who hold a different map to their own, even if the difference is slight. It is equally inevitable that people will experience elation or threat by interacting with other people. It all depends on the state of your map and the other party's map on meeting each other.

On this basis, politics in organisations is inevitable.

THE POLITICIANS

To further clarify the concept of politics, four stereotyped characters are analysed, based on the perception/action model (Figure 1.1): traditionalist, team coach, company baron and visionary.

Traditionalist

Traditionalists wish to fit in with the rest of the organisation. They accept the fact that they are dependent on the objectives provided by others. They accept the way resources are allocated, even if it is detrimental to their interests. If resources were allocated in the past in a particular way, then that is the way it ought to continue.

By sticking so much to the past, traditionalist-oriented people are concerned that others do likewise. Hence, they emphasise control of group membership, especially new people entering the group. Considerable time will be spent discussing other people's suitability to enter the group. Are they the right sort of person? Will they rock the boat? Do they dress appropriately? Most of all, do they look right? Once in the group, how do they behave? Traditionalist people will ensure that their group's identity and prevailing attitudes are not threatened with change or extinction for they pay particular attention to the way new members interact with the more established group members. If someone is seen to misbehave or try to act above his station, then some form of retribution will follow, usually a reprimand. In extreme cases, the erring individual would be threatened with expulsion from the group.

Despite their group orientation, traditionalists do not like warm, friendly relations. Their dominant concern is their role and status in their group. They strive to be 'top dog' over others. They would prefer to maintain superior/subordinate distance especially with subordinates. Becoming too close to people might mean losing status.

As far as work is concerned, traditionalists prefer to work on

Traditionalists in the cockpit, but in the boardroom?

It is easy to see how airline pilots can develop strong traditionalist attitudes. Most of their professional lives are spent in a small, confined space, surrounded by instrumentation, with only a few people to supervise directly. Understandably, accomplishment at technical skills and small group supervisory skills are highly valued. Equally understandably, accountants, administrators and managers are considered at best unnecessary and at worst a nuisance. After all, what do they know about flying?

Traditionalists may be all right in the cockpit, but not in the boardroom. However, a major world airline company reported a substantial loss in 1981 and in 1982. One wonders where the traditionalists are situated. The airline's chief executive has publicly laid blame on external factors, such as the air traffic controllers' strike in the Spring of 1981; the recession; rising fuel costs (aggravated by a strong dollar); government interference etc.

Certainly, external factors have aggravated the situation. In reality, the old familiar story of a large, inefficient, protected industry having to face intense competition during a period of industrial recession is nearer the truth. Amongst world airlines, this particular company rates high in terms of number of people employed, but only middle of the scale in terms of output as measured by tons carried for kilometres flown. To achieve anything near profitability, the company needs to make redundant 15,000 employees. Further, around 450 pilots out of a total of 3,000 are surplus to current requirements. The surplus reflects not only cutbacks in the number of flights but also the introduction of new aircraft requiring two flying crew as opposed to three. The problem is further exacerbated by a real lack of integration between various parts of the company. A wasteful duplication of resources and systems have been in operation for some time.

A large, traditional, divided organisation did not account for certain contingencies. The cuts the airline is imposing on itself may save the company, but they are drastic. People will be hurt, but the problems could have been foreseen.

details and be closely supervised by someone they trust and respect. That someone should have been a member of the organisation for some time and not be too young. Young people coming up the organisation are considered a threat and disliked. Not only does the traditionalist want his group/unit/department to stay the same, but also wants it to stay the same in its status and position to the rest of the organisation] Any reorganisation that takes place could be seen as threatening, even if it does not directly affect the traditionalist's group. His concern is – when will it be us?

Although traditionalist are conservative, inflexible and fearful of change (especially changes of group leadership), they do play a vital role in organisations. Their preference to work on detailed tasks is of great advantage for they will complete all the tiresome jobs others would not wish to do.

Further, their link with the past provides for stability in the organisation. They tend to be loyal to each other and to the organisation. It is ironic that when changes occur, their loyalty and hard work are not rewarded. The very people previously in demand are now no longer needed. No wonder they are fearful of changes of situation and leadership.

Traditionalists can tolerate each other. As stated, what they cannot tolerate is dramatic or unexpected change or people who are very different to themselves (i.e. company barons and visionaries). When confronted with one or either, traditionalists show a high concern that the organisation could deteriorate. They hold a pathological attitude: 'why is it that things were always better in the past?'

Team coach

The team coach develops his own ideas and beliefs as to how he would wish to conduct his life and affairs. However, independence of thought is not matched by independence of action. The team coach does need to belong to a group of like-minded people and may spend some time searching for a group with which he wishes to associate. On becoming members of a group, team coaches may see themselves as missionaries, whose calling is to shift the predominant values of the organisation nearer to the values of the group. The team coach would be sincere in his attempts to help others in the organisation experience the same degree of work satisfaction as he does with his team/group or unit.

In contrast to the traditionalist, the team coach pays substantial attention to nurturing warm, informal, personal relationships, especially to newcomers in the group. They would be made to feel welcome and their induction to the group would be a comfortable experience. Relationships in the group are likely to be conducted on a first-name basis.

The team coach would try to ensure that his group is satisfied and content. Anyone who indicated dissatisfaction would be given plenty of attention in an attempt to improve their situation. Anyone who was constantly disruptive within the group would probably be asked, politely, to leave. If the person did not leave, then the others in the group would be urged to ignore them.

A group of bright, energetic team coaches can together make for an innovative team. They do have the capacity for independent thinking and generating new ideas. Team coaches do seek a task orientation to their work. Rather than being concerned with their personal role or status, team coaches would aim to provide goods, products or services of high quality. Their role position in the organisation would be considered a relatively unimportant concern. They would find it acceptable to see their role altered if it led to product or service improvement. Team coaches take pleasure in applying their skills to certain new and exciting areas of work.

Hence, the team coach is far more flexible than the traditionalist. He can accept changes of role or status, job content and even changes of resource allocation as long as there are no significant upsets in his group/unit as a result. As long as the group remains intact, change can be seen as a challenge. Once changes upset the structure of the group or its position in the organisation, team coaches would act together to prevent any further changes taking place. Team coaches are flexible to the extent that they are stimulated by interacting with people who think and feel differently to them. However, their need for consistency of behaviour prevents any real change of group opinion and hence any substantial innovation in tasks. Task accomplishment comes to be doing what you were good at before but always a little better.

Similar to the traditionalists, team coaches can become over-concerned about changes that take place in the organisation.

Unlike traditionalists, team coaches are unlikely to display the same loyalty to the organisation. They are likely to display far greater loyalty to their group. If sufficiently threatened, they may leave the organisation *en masse* or shortly after one another, to seek another job. The team coach got his name from the interviews conducted with soccer coaches. It was recognised that certain people can cope with unshared meaning but insist on consistency of behaviour.

How the team coach got his name

I have observed and held a series of interviews with both soccer players and the coaches of particular soccer teams about their life and work. The coach of each team was especially interesting. He was a different sort of person from both the manager and the players.

The coach was surprisingly liberal in attitude. Most coaches held no prejudices concerning the colour, race or religion of their players. As long as the individual could play soccer, the coach was happy.

Certain coaches at the beginning of the interviews gave an impression that they disliked people with university degrees or who were intellectual in any way. The impression was false. Certain players were already quite well academically qualified and others had committed themselves to taking part-time degrees or professional qualifications. As far as the coach was concerned, if the player gave his all to the team, then the individual could, in his own time, pursue whatever interests he wished.

Most of the coaches stated in interviews that above all they respected talent on the football field. Each coach had his own hero(es) and would spend much time explaining the skills of his chosen model player. He would compare players in the existing first and second teams and rate them with his hero player. Not unexpectedly, most of the players in no way compared with the stars of yesteryear.

In practice, the coach was most concerned about team unity. Outside the soccer club, each player could think and do what they liked. Within the team, cohesion was most important. Understandably so, for it is the team that wins matches, not particular individuals. Anyone seen to disrupt the team would be first dealt with in a hard but paternalistic manner. If that did not work, then harsher methods could be used, such as sending him to the manager for a reprimand or advising the manager that the player should not be selected for the first team. In certain clubs, the coach and the manager were one and the same person. In such situations, the manager would try to behave as two people, as a coach to his players and as a manager and disciplinarian to the club.

A positive team spirit was so vital to develop and maintain that other factors could be sacrificed in order to generate a well-

> balanced team. Certain players at other clubs who were recog-
> nised for their high level of skill would not be considered suitable
> to buy as they were thought to be temperamentally unfitting or
> too individualistic. Gifted players were only recognised as
> valuable if they could be moulded into the existing team.
>   The reason why certain coaches were suspicious of univer-
> sity graduates was that the educated person was seen as
> questioning too much. The coach felt threatened. In one club in
> the north of England, certain players threatened industrial
> action as a way of having their grievances met. The most vocal of
> the players were the graduates. At that particular club, graduates
> mean trouble.

Company baron

The company baron has two dominant characteristics: an
ability to see the total organisation as it really is; and a
continuous strong drive to enhance his position and, if need be,
emphasise and amplify his role at the expense of others.

Both the company baron and the visionary share one strong
characteristic; the insight to develop a 'bird's eye view' of their
organisation. The skill of both types is their capacity to think
and conceptualise in whole organisational terms. They seem to
be able to foresee potential problems in the organisation. For
example, if the organisation were to market new services or
products, the company baron and the visionary would attempt
to predict the repercussions such moves would have on the
organisation. Hence, both types seem to be able to recognise
quickly how resources are really allocated in the organisation,
who to influence to get what they want and what are the unspoken
norms and values in the organisation that should never be
challenged.

However, that is where the similarities between the two types
cease. Although the company baron has considerable insight
into how things are really done and why, what he finds difficult
is to disengage or become separate from the majority in the
organisation. As a result, the company baron rarely attempts to
introduce large-scale changes into the organisation which
would involve shifts of organisational values and changes of
structure. More than likely, he would examine the performance
of particular divisions/departments/units/work systems in
order to make any necessary alterations. One fact is sure: the
company baron would never do something unless it suited his
purposes.

The company baron is likely to practise two political styles in
the organisation. On one side, he would constantly manoeuvre
to ensure he had the upper hand whilst on the other, he would

support the traditionalists of the organisation and champion values such as loyalty, hard work and patronage. The self-oriented style would mean the company baron would be conscious of his status in the organisation. He would attempt to enhance his role and become involved in the various power struggles in the organisation as long as his role and position are not harmed. The company baron makes an excellent committee politician.

The fact that he is outer-directed and shares the values and norms of the organisation is a good measure of his commitment to work within the existing systems. He is likely to be efficient at working on the smallest details as well as tackling larger issues and organising the necessary parties to make their contribution to any project. His style is to collaborate with others and usually seek their opinion before making his move. He needs others on his side before action is taken. His working towards gathering support from others could be misinterpreted as sitting on the fence.

The company baron plays an important role in the organisation. He has the ability to gather together various individuals and groups of differing vested interests and help them work towards particular objectives. Some may dislike his self-centred role and status orientation but that is outweighed by his capacity to work at the pace of others who are not united in their objectives, without leaving any stones unturned. In achieving medium and long-term strategy plans, the company baron is a vital link.

Despite his administrative skills, the company baron will only seek to introduce evolutionary change. Typically, he has probably been part of the organisation for some time. He may even have 'grown up' in the system. He will have identified with the old values of the organisation. He would have known many of the people who have stayed there for any length of time. Hence, his commitment to the established values of the organisation and his personal knowledge of the people in it makes it psychologically impossible for him to introduce dramatic change. He is unable to distance himself from the past.

As indicated, the company baron shares the values of maintaining traditions, patronage, honesty and hard work. He could easily dislike people who would 'rock the boat' with too many bright ideas or too many demands for change. He may be in favour of conducting more intellectual discussions as long as they do not become intense and they do not result in active demands for change and re-organisation.

The company baron is a difficult individual to handle. On the one side, his need for power and self-gain makes it difficult to control him or even to predict his next move. On the other, his capacity for loyalty to the organisation makes him a valuable asset. He provides a fatherly stability, coupled with a good appreciation of present and future problems.

In a sense, a number of company barons together cancel each other out. One is unlikely to let any other become King. In addition, with their sense of oneness with the organisation, they are unlikely to destroy the kingdom if they do not get what they want.

The company baron at his best

The managing director (MD) of a subsidiary of a multinational chemical company attended a week's seminar on creativity and lateral thinking at Head Office. He returned feeling enthusiastic that something creative should be done in his company which he hoped would become a profitable venture.

The MD contacted two management academics at an established business school and explained that he wanted to organise some sort of creativity seminar in the company but the ultimate objective would be to identify some new and exciting venture in which the company could invest and develop. The two management academics agreed to help and act as creativity consultants.

After prolonged negotiations between the management academics and the MD, it was finally decided that the company should gather its twelve brightest managers for two days a month, for the next few months, to attend creativity seminars. The two academic consultants were not involved in the selection of the twelve bright stars.

The first two-day seminar was held at a hotel in Manchester (UK). The academic consultants ran a number of creativity exercises simply to acquaint the participants with the subject of creativity. On the second day of the seminar a number of sub-groups was created to brainstorm new ideas. The consultants recognised that the main topic of discussion was not new ideas for the future but rather how to improve the existing systems and administration in the organisation. At the end of the two days, the participants stated that they thoroughly enjoyed themselves. A second seminar was arranged, to be held in London one month hence.

The two consultants considered the first seminar relatively successful. They held credibility with the group, the participants enjoyed themselves and were looking forward to the next seminar. The consultants, however, found one potentially disturbing factor. Virtually everyone had talked about just improving the current situation. No new ideas, no matter how unreal, were offered.

At the next seminar, just a few creativity/lateral thinking exercises were introduced. For most of the two days the participants were placed in their sub-groups to brainstorm and develop new ideas for the future. The two consultants played an active role as catalysts to help the participants generate new ideas, no matter how absurd. The participants again presented the same sort of practical ideas on how to improve the present systems. On this occasion, the seminar fell a little flat.

However, a third seminar was arranged one month hence. The two consultants asked the participants to make an effort to keep in touch with one another so as to exchange the ideas and keep the issues alive during the month's absence. At the third seminar much the same occurred – few ideas were generated. The consultants switched the team around but that made little difference.

The consultants requested an interview with the MD. They indicated to him that the seminars were not working out. Some useful suggestions had emerged but not the sort of ideas the MD wanted. The consultants suggested that they pick out twelve other candidates in the company to take part in the seminars. The MD agreed. After a three-month search, twelve likely and willing participants were found. The list of twelve names was presented to the MD for his approval. The MD was shocked. He considered most of the new group of twelve to be trouble-makers and what was worse they were seen as intelligent trouble-makers. They were always wanting to change things. The consultants argued that they felt these to be the ones with the new and innovative ideas. The MD stated that he wanted evolution not revolution and that the original twelve would continue as the inspirational source of new ideas.

After further negotiations with the MD, the consultants felt they could no longer make a contribution to the project and withdrew. Two months later, one of the consultants met, quite by chance, one of the project team members at a railway station in London. After a brief exchange of pleasantries, the consultant asked how the project had developed.

'OK. We have disbanded', was the reply. 'The MD got everything he wanted'.

The consultant asked his companion to explain. Apparently, the original idea for creativity came from the group chief executive. The MD of this subsidiary, aiming for the favour of the chief executive and the main board, set about to show that creativity training could work and produce practical results. The MD also recognised that too revolutionary ideas would not be acceptable. He wanted people to think of ways of improving the system. The ideas of the creativity group were just right. The MD took them to the main board to show how creativity could work.

The consultants' withdrawal turned out to be a blessing in disguise for the MD. He argued at the main board that he could dispense with the services of outsiders fairly quickly as he was well capable of managing the process himself. After all, the results spoke for themselves.

Visionary

As stated, the visionary, similar to the company baron, possesses an ability to see the organisation in total. Although he can think and conceptualise in whole organisational terms, the visionary does not feel the same need for loyalty to the organisation. Hence, not only can the visionary question and examine the way resources are allocated in the organisation and explore what are suitable structures for the organisation, but he can also stand back from the values, views and stereotypes held by the majority in the organisation. Such independence of mind is invaluable if faced with re-organisation and re-structuring.

Visionary-oriented people tend to operate from their visions of the future concerning the organisation and the world outside. They have particular, personal values as to how things ought to be done and beliefs about what will happen in the future. Coupled with their ability to conceptualise organisations in whole terms, they are able to predict which parts of the organisation require alteration and adjustment in order to achieve certain long-term objectives. Sir Geoffrey Vickers (1968) described such people as possessing 'systemic wisdom' – having a clear insight into how long-term trends in the world outside will affect the organisation.

As visionary people develop their own personalised visions and beliefs about the future, and their own philosophies about work and strategies for action, they tend to operate in relative isolation from others. Such philosophies tend to be a personal expression of self; their identity; what they stand for, all which have been generated in isolation from others and hence are difficult to share with others. Sharing personal values is difficult. It is hard to co-operate with someone who has the ability to develop equally well-formed ideas that are different (or even similar) but stem from separate personal values. In-fighting between board members of companies can be the result of such fundamental differences of opinion. Usually, there is little room for compromise unless one party surrenders. Often, battles amongst visionaries are conducted in an undercover, cloak and dagger way with little animosity shown on the surface. If such battles go on for too long, it is possible that the organisation may suffer in terms of forward planning. Usually one of the warring parties has to leave. It is the visionary's ability to interpret current events, predict future trends and generate an alternative identity that makes his view of the world unique. It is a matter of 'two into one won't go'.

However, it is to the advantage of the visionary to share with others how fundamental strategies, once decided, should be implemented. The involvement of others not only ensures that strategies are put into practice but allows them to identify with the new values, attitudes and norms of behaviour in the re-structured organisation. Whether others approve of the new changes or not, the visionary would seek to introduce more dramatic change. He would not value planned, step-by-step change as he is not committed to the previous values and structure of the organisa-tion. In his day-to-day style, the visionary would be far less cautious than the company baron in playing politics and introducing changes. He will 'test the water' before making his move but will not be too dependent on the support of others. Rather, he would use his influencing skills to state his case. He would use his interpersonal skills to influence individuals before and after meetings. During meetings, he would probably be more assertive than the company baron and be prepared to handle any conflict that is directed towards him. On the whole, the visionary is more prepared to risk.

The visionary toy maker

It must have been quite a surprise for Mr Karl Mueller, the current managing director of Hornby (the toy train company) to be in 1980 invited, with other managers, to a meeting in London only to be introduced to the receivers. Hornby was then part of the Dunbee–Combex–Marx toy group which collapsed in early 1980 with debts of around £19m. Mueller went into action to save Hornby and the 1,400 skilled workforce. Mueller went round knocking on doors in the City of London, searching for cash to buy the company from the receiver. Not only were many doors slammed in his face; some did not even open.

Using the services of a stockbroker, Mueller eventually was backed by a consortium which included the Citibank and Electra Investment Trust, and they bought out Hornby from the receiver. Although Mueller feels it will still take two years to pull the company together, he was expecting a profit of over £1m before tax in 1982. As part of the drive to profitability, the company sees little scope for growth in the UK (its traditional market) and is now directing its efforts to overseas markets. Toy trains are popular in the UK, but not abroad. Mueller is setting about educating foreign markets. He has met with success in the Republic of Ireland. France has now been selected as the big spearhead area.

(Source: Financial Times, 15 December 1981)

Visionaries are a valuable asset in any organisation. Their drive, energy and flamboyance makes them attractive to others. Their new ideas, if properly harnessed, make an invaluable contribution to the development and growth of the organisation. However, visionaries are not easy to manage. If they are not doing something challenging, they could become bored, critical of management and the organisation and possibly leave. They may also feel constrained by the systems in the organisation and again be over-critical of management.

There tend to be few visionaries. Not unexpectedly, their skills are much in demand. Their capacity to rationalise in whole organisational terms and create fundamental, realistic and at times adventurous strategies for change and then work towards developing a series of inter-related tasks to match the original strategy, is unlikely to be developed through management training. They train themselves on the job.

Visionaries have been used as action men brought in at the top to re-vitalise an ailing organisation.

WHO AM I?

Nobody is just one type or has one style. All of us are a mixture of values, attitudes, styles of behaviour and particular skills that we practise.

One way to view the self is to arrange the components that form the make-up of a person in order of importance (Figure 1.2). Something that is uniquely you – the core you – is probably impossible to measure or define. However, there are other parts of us, such as values, attitudes and styles which we can examine.

What are your values? Are you outer-directed or inner-directed? What are the true determinants of your behaviour? Each person should be at least partially aware of what stimulates his actions and feelings. Having some insight into himself may help him cope better with stressful or unpleasant situations.

As far as attitudes are concerned, people are unlikely to have just one or one sort. They hold a number of different attitudes. Hence, people are likely to possess a combination of the simple–complex behaviour attitudes. The important question for each individual is which type of attitude predominates?

Further, do you find that there are certain attitudes others have which you cannot tolerate? What attitudes are those?

The combination of the predominant shared values and the

predominant attitudes of most people, form the acceptable and unacceptable norms of behaviour in the organisation. Over time, the norms become the traditions and the combination of traditions develop into the various cultures and the total climate of the organisation. The norms, traditions, cultures and climate are the guidelines as to what the organisation can and cannot accept; what attitudes and values will and will not be tolerated. For anyone who has to work in an organisation, it is important to remain within the boundaries of acceptability.

People exhibit their values and attitudes by their styles of interpersonal behaviours. Each individual is likely to exhibit more than one style of behaviour. Most people are likely to have one or two preferred styles. Some will only have a limited repertoire of styles they can call on. The more accomplished politician will have a wide repertoire. Further, he will know which style to use with what person and under what circumstances.

Skills refer to on-the-job performance standards. How effectively has a person performed? Skills could refer to the interpersonal skills of influencing people or to particular professional skills that may only have developed after years of training.

Can I change?

Yes, everyone can change, but to what depth and to what extent partly depends on why change of self is deemed necessary.

Change stimulated by a wish to improve one's performance is not only feasible but desirable. Changes or adaptation to one's personal styles, interpersonal influencing skills or even professional skills should not be too difficult to achieve.

However, for a change of style and skills to be effective, the individual should be prepared to make adjustments to his attitudes. Being trained in interpersonal skills is of little use unless they are practised. Practising new skills may immediately differentiate you from your peers. For traditionalists especially, there is little point in improving one's skills of interpersonal influence unless the objective is to influence numerous and varied people. The individual should, therefore, want to mix with different people. Should the person develop such skills, his peers will quickly notice the changes and also be sensitive to his change of attitude. It is common practice for management development managers to send line managers on one or two-week development courses in interpersonal skills, not just for them to learn new skills but also to experience a change of attitude towards their work, personal style, superior/subordinates and the organisation.

Changing oneself at the values level is more difficult. Rather than merely adjusting one's behaviour pattern to suit new and varied circumstances, more fundamental changes require that the individual re-assess his needs, desires and preferred activities.

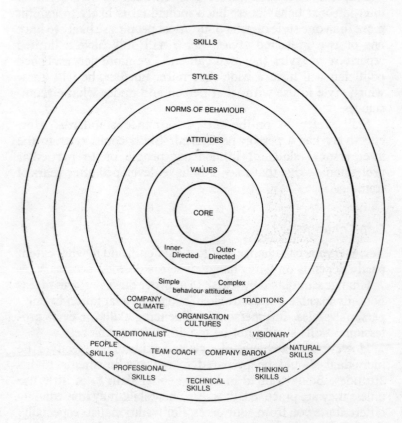

Figure 1.2   Viewing self and organisation *

---

*   This model was first developed by my good friend and colleague, Ralph Lewis, an exceptionally skilful teacher of management.

The individual is exploring his own attitudes and values without necessarily behaving in new and different ways. People often experience such fundamental re-examination when life begins to go wrong, e.g. divorce, redundancy, demotion or rejection. For the person concerned, the process is painful with no guarantee that the changes will be for the better.

Your repertoire of political styles

As stated, all people possess a repertoire of styles and skills, some being more accomplished than others. Complete the following questionnaire to identify your dominant and back-up interpersonal political styles.

The self-perception inventory

Below are 40 statements in 10 sections which relate to you. Each section comprises 4 statements.

For each section, distribute a total of 7 points which you think best describe you and your behaviour. You may, for example, wish to spread the 7 points amongst some or all of the 4 statements. Alternatively you may wish to place all 7 points on one statement. In your responses, try to be as honest as you can.

Once you have completed this procedure, enter the points in the 2 tables on pages 37 and 38.

1 A GOOD BOSS
    (a) ☐ avoids the use of power for its own sake,
    (b) ☐ is impersonal and sticks to the formal channels of communication,
    (c) ☒ is someone who lets me get on with the job,
    (d) ☐ keeps his distance.

2 A GOOD SUBORDINATE
    (a) ☐ is responsible and reliable,
    (b) ☐ complies with the duties of his job,
    (c) ☐ should be treated as a co-worker, contributing particular skills and abilities to the total team effort,
    (d) ☐ is someone who sticks with his team mates through thick and thin.

3 AT WORK
    (a) ☐ before I do something, I make sure my boss agrees,
    (b) ☐ I like to be with people who are creative and seem

   to be doing something new,
   (c) ☑ I feel I am able to stimulate good working
           relationships,
   (d) ☑ I feel it is important that senior management
           maintain their distance by sending directives from
           the top down, and in turn assess information that
           is fed up to them. In this way life is fair for
           everyone.
4 AT WORK
   (a) ☐ if the truth be known, I only really reward those
           people who like my ideas or suggestions,
   (b) ☐ I lose interest when projects get bogged down by
           lengthy decision-making processes,
   (c) ☒ I often find it easier to do a job myself than to get
           others to do it right,
   (d) ☐ in order to work effectively with people, it is
           important to get to know them personally.
5 AT WORK
   (a) ☐ any form of change or disruption is acceptable
       ⁿ when it comes to improving the standards of goods
           or services,
   (b) ☐ I am fed up with people who seem to know little
           about my job and yet try to get me to do things
           differently,
   (c) ☐ I do not mind changes as long as they are not too
           disruptive,
   (d) ☐ changes are acceptable as long as they are planned
       ₃ and orderly.
6 AT WORK
   (a) ☐ people work well together when the systems and
           procedures define the way they should work,
   (b) ☐ I tend to get annoyed with people who don't do
           things by the established procedures,
   (c) ☐ rules and regulations should be interpreted so as to
           accommodate different people's needs,
   (d) ☐ if I want something done, I take little notice of the
           rules and procedures and do what I want.
7 AT MEETINGS
   (a) ☐ I tend to keep quiet if I seem to be the only one
           who supports a particular idea or action,
   (b) ☐ I can't be bothered trying to convince people of
           something they don't want to accept,

(c) ☐ I try to make sure that people don't lose sight of the main objectives,

(d) ☐ I try to stimulate warm and friendly relationships with others.

8 FOR ME

(a) ☐ large-scale organisational changes are an opportunity for advancement,

(b) ☐ improving my status in the organisation is as important as being paid more money,

(c) ☐ going to work is important because of the people I meet,

(d) ☐ things should be kept the way they are.

9 I DISLIKE

(a) ☐ people who pursue personal power. They make me feel uneasy,

(b) ☐ people who question my suggestions or decisions,

(c) ☐ discussing and handling details,

(d) ☐ people who always seem to want to do something new.

10 AND FINALLY

(a) ☐ becoming part of the 'old boy' network is a good way of getting to the top,

(b) ☐ to take a risk and do something new, even though it may harm my position in the organisation, really turns me on,

(c) ☐ when all is said and done the only person I safely depend on is myself,

(d) ☐ I really don't mind what people think, as long as they don't upset others around them.

STATEMENT	a	b	c	d
1			X	
2	X	X	X	
3				
4				
5				
6				
7				
8				
9				
10				

Statement	Tradition-alist		Team coach		Company baron		Visionary	
1	d	*4*	a	*1*	b	*2*	c	*7*
2	b	*1*	d		a	*2*	c	*5*
3	a		c	*3*	d	*5*	b	
4	c	*7*	d		a		b	
5	b		c		d	*3*	a	*4*
6	b		c		a		d	
7	a		d		c		b	
8	d		c		b		a	
9	b		a		d		c	
10	c		d		a		b	
Total score								

The column with the highest score represents your most used style. The second highest score represents your back-up style, and so on.

Examine the spread of scores. If the difference in scores between your most preferred style and back-up style is high, (i.e. greater than 6), that indicates that you prefer to use that style most of the time. If the differences in scores are low between your most preferred style, back-up style or even a third style, it indicates you have a range of styles to call on to suit different circumstances.

2 How The Politicians Operate

How do the politicians operate? The question is explored in this chapter by examining the way the politicians control and co-ordinate activities; reward and motivate people; and influence and change their work environment.

THE TRADITIONALIST

Approaches to controlling and co-ordinating

For the traditionalist, the question is not how to control and co-ordinate activities, or even what to control and co-ordinate, but rather *whom* to control and co-ordinate. The traditionalist's predominant concern is group membership, particularly his/her group, and the current focal issues of the group. Who is and who is not in favour in the group; who is trying to do too much too quickly or not keeping pace with other members; who is involved in activities that could tarnish the image of the group in the eyes of its members, are all key concerns. For traditionalists control and co-ordination are applied when individual behaviour does not comply with group norms; when precedence is broken.

From the point of view of the traditionalist, irreverence for precedence means crisis. Not honouring accepted ways of doing things, upsetting the status quo, causing discomfort to the long-serving senior members of the group, indicates that a pathological situation has developed which must be put right.

To put things right, the traditionalist would give the unfortunate individual more work, supervise him closely, point to all his mistakes and offer reprimands, not become too emotionally involved and maintain his distance whilst dealing with the person. Through closely supervised, controlled work activities, group norm breakers are shown that the status quo is best.

'Spare the rod and spoil the child', is significant for the traditionalist. It matters little whether the 'child' is over 30 years of age. All transgressors have certain child-like qualities, which must be re-shaped to bring the person back to the fold.

The man in the middle

John had been a personnel consultant for over 19 years in the same consultancy company, 11 years of which he had spent working with the same team. A new team leader, Cedric, was appointed. After Cedric settled in, he suggested to John that experience with another team or even attending a short course would be beneficial. It would give John time off to develop and reflect on his consultant style and work practice. John, however, viewed Cedric's suggestion with suspicion – why should he want me to reflect on my style; after all, I have been doing the same good steady job for the last 11 years? John's suspicion grew to hostility. He tried to avoid Cedric and to present him with incomplete information which enhanced the position of John and at the same time attempted to ensure that Cedric had no access to his work.

Cedric considered John as out-of-date in terms of knowledge and work practice; as a person who attempted to prevent positive change within the work team; ineffective in client–consultant relationships and generally a symbol of passive resistance to Cedric's authority. The situation between the two deteriorated further. Cedric attempted to become more involved with John, whereas John attempted to avoid Cedric as much as possible. When avoidance became impossible, John entered into defensive hostile behaviours such as not presenting work for supervision, not regularly attending group meetings, questioning Cedric's actions and sending unpleasant memos about Cedric's behaviour to both his friends in the team and in other teams.

Cedric talked about John to the divisional director – Alan – a long-standing company employee who had known John for some time. Alan counselled Cedric to be understanding, talk more to John and if necessary leave him alone. Cedric attempted Alan's recommendations but found that there was no change in John's behaviour. Things became calmer when Cedric left John alone. For Cedric that was a sign of failure.

Finally, Cedric did rid himself of John by appointing him abroad and manoeuvring him to a position where John opted for early retirement. Unfortunately, shortly after John retired, Cedric was eased out by his own superior. Alan told Cedric, 'see how you like your own medicine.'

When group norms are not threatened, there is little need for the traditionalist to act. The existing system should take account of most contingencies. The traditionalist will have given a great deal of effort to developing a system that would control and co-ordinate work-oriented activities, as well as the behaviour of group members. In the case above, Cedric had not fully appreciated that both John and Alan were traditionalists. For both of them, acting on change, joint decision making and thinking about the future were a virtual impossibility. Cedric made three errors that eventually cost him his job. First, he tried to get John to co-ordinate himself instead of controlling and closely supervising him from the start. Second, he attempted to carry out Alan's advice of being open, friendly and caring about John, not realising that he had not known John long enough to establish a warmer relationship. Trying to be more open made matters worse, for John became even more suspicious. Third, Cedric had not fully appreciated that his boss, Alan, was as traditionalist as John. Threaten John and you threaten Alan, which meant Cedric had to go.

Approaches to rewarding and motivating

Effective communication and comfortable interpersonal interaction have to be achieved before the traditionalist attempts to reward and motivate others. For communication to be effective, it has to be conducted formally through memo or pre-arranged meetings. Throughout the interaction it is important to maintain superior/subordinate distance, maintain an air or formality and ensure that the traditionalist does not see himself as losing face in the encounter.

If the traditionalist is allowed to operate in a structured environment, given direction in the tasks he/she performs, allowed to work on routine and established procedures, then the individual has been sufficiently motivated to, in turn, motivate others. Unlike the other politicians, the traditionalist requires to feel secure before he will give his attention to others. There are two motivators the traditionalist can offer: his approval and favour; and invitation to continued membership of the group.

By adhering to the values and beliefs of the traditionalist, other people will be rewarded by his paternalistic approval. Such approval is hard to gain. The traditionalist in turn would expect the other party to exhibit thanks for the recognition and a willingness to continue with further good work.

If not already a member, the individual may be invited to join the traditionalist's group. If already a member, the individual's position in the group is assured. If held in high favour, the person may be offered the special honour of becoming a member of the inner circle.

Approaches to influencing and changing

In a world where adherence to group norms becomes life goals, attempts at influence and change are concerned with achieving no change – maintaining the status quo.

Consider what is likely to happen when changes at work are being contemplated. People may form groups to discuss ideas and developments for the future, involve others in making decisions and supervise the activities of those on poorly structured tasks. Such interaction is likely to be resisted by the traditionalist, as it stimulates great discomfort for him. In response, he may not attend project group meetings, reject people's recommendations and complain that he cannot do a good job as so many changes are confusing and he no longer knows where he stands. The traditionalist may well ask why he should be involved in making decisions that may have previously been the prerogative of senior management? He may argue that motivating and developing people and situations is best achieved by no change.

At worst, the traditionalist could react adversely if the unity of his group is threatened. He would find it difficult to cope if he were personally criticised or challenged. Such processes would lead him to reject all recent events as unwelcome change.

Those who can do, those who can't .....?

It was considered by most staff members of a department of management of a well-known British polytechnic that new approaches to management training had to be introduced to the department's training portfolio. Student numbers had been slowly dropping over the past two years and the department faced the prospect of having its budget reduced unless it attracted more students.

The head of department held a series of meetings asking staff members whether they had any suggestions. From about half the staff members the response was 'it's your problem! Our job is to teach; your job is to bring in the people whom we shall teach.' From the other half came a series of suggestions about how to improve existing programmes and what new programmes should be considered. However, all the suggestions had one factor in common – all staff members wanted formal lecture-type programmes.

One junior member of staff offered an entirely different idea, that of generating action learning-type programmes whereby managers could use the department's facilities to meet and discuss their work problems. Formal training programmes would be replaced by semi-structured discussions of work problems, managed by the managers themselves.

The suggestion was rejected on the grounds that managers who were not given anything to do would criticise the department and hence potential customers could be lost. The junior staff member persisted, arguing that nothing could be more attractive to managers than to discuss themselves, share experiences and solve their own problems. The staff member persisted to such an extent that the head of the department and others not in favour of the idea, gave way.

The idea was adopted but not in the way the junior staff member envisaged. The responsibility for establishing action learning programmes was given to a more senior staff member. He was told that if the programme was to be acceptable, each member of staff involved would have to be given X number of teaching credits for their contribution. The most feasible way of equitably awarding teaching credits was to organise a structured teaching programme, where the lecturers would be credited for every hour they taught on the programme.

The programme was advertised and initially generated a substantial response. Within the first two weeks, student numbers dropped. On one occasion, a vociferous mature student complained to the head of department that the action learning programme was marketed as something new. From the student's position, he could not tell the difference between the new programme and any of the standard diploma in management studies programmes. The head of department said he would do something, but did nothing.

Two years on, the programme has been dropped due to lack of student numbers. The department is still losing students every year.

The department was dominated by traditionalists.

Whatever new was to be done, the way it was done had to be similar to the way things were previously done. The very reason change was needed was that the lecturing approach to training managers was considered inappropriate by the consumers. Yet the view genuinely held by the staff was that change must comply with the existing administration. In fact, most staff members did not even wish to discuss change. For the remainder, change consisted of doing things in much the same way as before.

Only one person stood out and argued vociferously for something new. In order to maintain group cohesion, his suggestion was adopted. However, he was dropped from further discussions and the proposal turned into something that was acceptable to the group. For traditionalists, the need to maintain the status quo blocks any innovative re-examination of current systems and structures.

The head of department, today, still does not fully appreciate why he cannot attract the required number of students.

THE TEAM COACH

Approaches to controlling and co-ordinating

Unlike the traditionalists, the team coach understands that strictly maintaining the status quo is an impossible long-term

---

Team coach in R and D

The assistant vice-president of an R and D department in a US aerospace organisation left for a more lucrative post in another organisation. A quiet unassuming senior member of the R and D department was offered the vacated post, which he accepted.

Most people in the department considered him to be uninspiring, boring, dull and certainly not a leader of a group of innovative people. One or two of the members of the department even complained to the president of the organisation that the appointment was a poor one. However, the appointment stood.

Shortly, people's views of the new man changed. His quiet, unassuming manner became a positive advantage. People recognised him as a warm, feeling individual, who was most attentive to the problems of his departmental colleagues. Most in the department felt secure with him as departmental chief. He provided stability. Soon, most members in the department began to compare him with the previous chief. The previous chief was considered brilliant, innovative but a somewhat unsettling influence. The previous chief was a workaholic and expected others to achieve a similar work output. People who did not perform to his very high standards stood no chance of promotion or increases in pay. Although most members of the department respected the previous chief's abilities, no-one liked him as a person and most considered his managerial style as uncompromising and authoritarian.

The new chief soon became the department's favourite. Most people would talk to him and felt comfortable in discussing more personal issues. Only one person has exhibited dissatisfaction with the new situation. One of the more alert and energetic R and D scientists simply wondered when they were all going to get back to doing some new, exciting work. Having someone you can talk to is alright, but what about some strong leadership to achieve good output?

objective. The team coach appreciates that working with people who think and feel differently to oneself is necessary for the continued development and growth of the organisation.

The team coach will depend less on close control of detailed work or offers of reprimand for misdemeanours committed, but be more understanding and sympathetic, and he will develop rapport with group members or even non-group members. The team coach will depend more on his interpersonal skills in order to develop meaningful and workable relationships with others. He/she will pay less attention to the details of work and more to the person and how he feels. In fact, the team coach will go out of his way to become acquainted with new members of the group, or, if seen relevant, new members of the organisation.

The aim of the team coach is to develop consensual patterns of decision making in the group. In this way, people will be in tune with the group and its objectives. In order to achieve this, the team coach will allow for changes of work patterns, more flexible working hours and changes in the resources allocated to different group members.

For the team coach, control and co-ordination become more oriented towards co-ordination, whether in times of crisis or calm.

The boxed case study on p. 44 ('Team coach in R and D') illustrates that the new chief is a team coach. His appointment seems to have been a wise move considering that a period of stability was needed after the leadership of a highly innovative, energetic, but uncompromising man. However, in the long run what impact will the new chief make? The case is current so it is impossible to say. Yet the warning signs are there. Simply paying attention to interpersonal processes may not be sufficient.

Approaches to rewarding and motivating

Team coaches reward and motivate others in two ways: through group membership and praise for task accomplishment.

The team coach much prefers more open, informal approaches to communication. Establishing rapport, integrating with others and attempting to generate an open climate, where both people problems and work problems could be genuinely and unashamedly discussed, would be the team coach's objective.

Therein lies one strong reward and motivational stimulus – be open and become integrated. The objective is to establish consensual decision-making patterns in the group. By generating a climate of openness, trust and rapport with the group, the team coach helps group members to identify with group norms. Such a process leads to further reward and motivation, for eventually group members are themselves generating the new group norms and not just adhering to them.

In terms of tasks and day-to-day work, praise from a well-respected team coach is reward in itself. Anyone strongly involved in the group of which he is a member may well find colleagues' praise for a job well done, a strong positive stimulus.

It should be remembered that integrating into the team/unit/department or group is as important as task accomplishment. Rewards are given to those who are good at their job and fit well with their peers. People who show themselves to be competent but make little or no attempt to integrate will be seen as troublesome. No matter how good they are, if they do not become part of the group, they will be ignored or even actively rejected.

Approaches to influencing and changing

The team coach would take a flexible position to change provided it did not unduly disrupt his team/unit/group/department. Changes of detail can be both tolerated and welcomed, as long as people in the group do not feel threatened. The team coach would also look to the position of his group in relation to other groups in the organisation. If the group is faced with a change of budget, all is well as long as other groups in the organisation face the same prospect. Disturbing the balance between groups would generate stress amongst team coaches.

Changes of task and work load would be acceptable provided the situation is discussed and matters agreed to in the group. Hence, the team coach would use his influencing skills to enter into discussions about change in the group, co-operate with supervisors, interact with colleagues and subordinates and generally be prepared to enter into debates about ideas for the future without personally experiencing discomfort.

Although team coaches can tolerate change as long as constancy is maintained, they are reactive by nature. They will discuss the ideas with others but at the same time are unwilling to lead the way and introduce substantial change. It is a mistake to assume that being co-operative and willing to participate are also signs of being able to be proactive. The team coach may take part in discussions, but may not be competent at decision making nor personally able to provide support for the change agent when the going gets rough.

The team coach who over-sold himself

George wanted the job with that US insurance company. The job was acting as internal consultant to senior management and the main board. The challenge was that the company wished to introduce changes of organisation structure, hire new people, provide better training, even diversify into new areas of business; all in preparation for the 1990s.

George wanted the job; for him, his experience seemed just right – management trainer, management consultant and in his last job, in charge of a management development unit in a subsidiary of a major multinational company.

George got the job. Senior managers and main board members congratulated him.

'Liked the way you handled yourself throughout all the interviews', said some.

'You know, George, we made the right choice', said others. George felt good!

Nine months on, George was not feeling so good. The president and one or two other senior managers asked George to explore the implications of entering into new areas of business. George's reports were not too good. The more polite senior managers said nothing. The president said his report was a 'load of balls'.

'I thought you said you knew something about business, George!' stormed the president.

One sympathetic senior manager politely took George through the report suggesting areas for improvement.

George, however, made some good recommendations concerning management training. He ran one or two programmes and showed how skilful he was at handling managers in the classroom.

George also showed to the main board members that they could improve the quality of their meetings. He sat in on their meetings and made helpful comments about the way different personalities interacted, how people were not listening to each other and offered helpful tips on how particular individuals could improve their interpersonal style.

However, when it came to business matters, George kept his mouth shut. All noticed his lack of contribution on the business development side of the company. A number of board members became irritated by his lack of contribution. One finally said, 'Look George, you seem to know a lot about people, but nothing about business. We hired you because you said you could handle both. What the hell are you going to do about it?'

George felt so bad, he could not reply. After a period of silence, the embarrassed chairman of the meeting suggested they continue with the business at hand. As soon as the meeting finished, George left; the others stayed.

'For Christ's sake, get George out of here. He is not only a pain

> in the arse to us, he is a pain in the arse to himself. Put him out of
> his misery and make him a damn training manager or something,'
> said one of the more outspoken board members.
>   'I think he is a genuine person. But I think you are right.
> George should be offered something more suitable,' said the
> president.
>   'About damn time', said the board member.

George is now a training manager and shares a secretary with
somebody else. He likes the people he works with. They all feel
senior management are bastards.

THE COMPANY BARON

Approaches to controlling and co-ordinating

The company baron has two aims; first, to improve his position
in the organisation; second, to improve the organisation now
and for the future but without upsetting its fundamental
traditions and values.

The company baron would attempt to improve his position in
the organisation by enhancing his role, even to the detriment of
others. How others view the company baron, his role and status
in the organisation, are key concerns. Consequently approaches
to control and co-ordination focus around role and status
considerations. Control measures are predominantly applied to
the activities of subordinates. Have subordinates followed
appropriate procedures? Have subordinates liaised or kept in
touch with appropriate individuals? Have subordinates behaved in a manner respectful to the position and status of
others? Attempts at control are there to ensure that subordinates work within the formal and informal, but well-understood
role constraints. In applying control, the company baron will
attempt to maintain superior/subordinate distance.

However, the company baron will not just attempt to fall in
line with existing role constraints. By ensuring that subordinates do not upset the status quo, the company baron is more
confident at interacting with people who may not think and feel
as himself. Again, co-ordinative activities are determined by
established procedures and roles. The company baron will enter
into lengthy decision-making processes, by arguing for policies
on committees and working parties. During debate and dis-

cussion, the company baron is unlikely to stick rigidly to a policy, but both adjust his behaviour and objectives to suit other people. Working within role and procedural constraints, finding compromises and ensuring that subordinates do not upset others in the system are all carefully orchestrated attempts at manoeuvring for increased personal power. The company baron recognises that it is necessary to work with others in the organisation different to oneself, but in order to have one's objectives accepted, one must be seen as powerful and influential.

Yet, all this manoeuvring is not just for self-oriented reasons. The company baron does attempt to re-appraise and adapt his organisation to accommodate future needs but within the traditions and basic structure of the organisation. To influence and control strategic changes within the organisation, ironically, the company baron favours co-ordination of people and activities as opposed to direct control.

Co-ordination would take place by interacting with others on numerous working parties and committees. Attempts at large-scale change would only be conducted through the existing committee and decision-making structures. In addition, the company baron would spend substantial time and effort on co-ordinating and interacting with his senior managers in order to develop a climate of comradeship at high levels. He, in turn, would encourage his senior managers to behave in a like manner with their subordinates and their teams.

Whereas co-ordination would be the tactic to stimulate positive, acceptable changes, attempts at direct control would only be practised if certain unexpected or unwelcomed aspects of change developed in the organisation. Certain people may be introducing too many changes too quickly; generating too many ideas too quickly; breaking precedence. That someone would simply be stopped. That someone is in danger of upsetting the spirit of tradition that has made the organisation successful.

Approaches to rewarding and motivating

The key issues for the company baron are role and status. Hence, the pattern of interaction that the baron develops with others is strongly influenced by concerns about *how others view me*. With subordinates, the company baron is likely to behave formally, ensuring they complete their allocated tasks and behave respectfully towards him. If the subordinate is competent at his job and further behaves in a respectfully appropriate way, rewards will be given in terms of increased pay and/or arguing on his behalf for promotion.

Patronage is the ultimate reward offered by the company baron. Favour is given to safe but talented individuals. Those who wish to court such favours should be aware that to be given such attention takes time. The ambitious individual has to plan for becoming involved in lengthy decision-making processes, being invited by the company baron to argue for key issues, accepting heavy responsibility as a reward in itself and working towards changes in the organisation through existing committee and decision-making structures. It is important to have been a member of the organisation for some time. An individual working his way up from the bottom is the most acceptable. A talented outsider entering at middle or senior management levels is in danger of being rejected as the company baron senses that he may display little loyalty to him and the traditional values.

In acting as godfather, the company baron uses promotion rewards as a form of control. The company baron always needs to feel that it is he who decides who is promoted or transferred to another position. Should the subordinate openly attempt to influence the direction of his promotion, he could lose the company baron's support.

Patterns of interaction with colleagues and superiors are somewhat different. With those with whom the company baron is not well acquainted, a position of formality is likely to be maintained. He may communicate through memos and discuss business at pre-arranged meetings. However, once that barrier has been broken down, the company baron may well invite those others to join his circle of socially acceptable acquaintances outside the work situation. For the company baron to offer, and be offered, such a reward is viewed as an important step forward. Such a strategy of interaction makes sense. Nothing enhances the role and status position of an individual more than developing a network of people who are likely to support him in his actions. Further, such a network is an efficient way of establishing people's views on certain issues. In this way, the company baron can plan in the knowledge that he can quickly get inside information and yet not upset too many people.

Handling the company baron, so you can do what you want

A female management development manager working for a large food products organisation in the USA wished to introduce new ways of training and developing the company's middle managers and senior executives. She had carefully prepared and documented her proposal indicating the benefits the company could expect from investing in new approaches to management development. She also indicated that her ideas were backed by a study of management needs recently conducted in the company by outside consultants. In her opinion, the study identified areas of weakness that she had recognised for some time.

Her proposals were put before her boss, vice president of personnel, who held a main board position. He refused to accept the proposals and further refused to allow them to be debated on the board. No firm explanation as to his reaction was given. The management development manager re-submitted the plans after alteration and was again refused permission to implement them. She tried twice again but was unsuccessful.

She approached me, stating her problem and asking whether I, as a consultant, could help form a better relationship between her and her boss. On further discussion, we established fairly clearly that her boss seemed to behave as a company baron and she as visionary. I urged her to present her case in a way that would be more acceptable to her boss. I suggested that she should emphasise his rise in status if the new project was to be accepted; its slender chances of failure and generally approach her boss in such a way that some of the ideas, although hers, could be made to seem as if they came from him.

She accepted my advice and re-submitted the package emphasising the status and role benefits her boss would gain and minimising the innovative ideas she had generated. The plan was accepted and is now in operation. It is seen by the rest of the board as a successful venture. The one drawback is that the management development manager is currently frustrated with her work situation. She feels she had not been given sufficient recognition for her efforts as her boss has attracted most of the glory for himself.

The message is clear. In order to stimulate the company baron to improve performance, it must be done in ways meaningful to him. Part of the process of influence involves proving not to be a threat. If the new ideas are good, the company baron may adopt some or most of them as his own, a situation which the management development manager found frustrating. What she does not know, however, is that the company baron, in this case, has appreciated her good work. His reward for her is promotion and increased pay. In fact, the

promotion will take her to a managerial level that no other
woman has occupied in the history of the company. The reason
the company baron is stalling is that he does not know how she
will react to his patronage. He wants her to show further loyalty
for such rewards. He does not want her to say, 'about damn
time. I should have got this promotion some time ago!'

Approaches to influencing and changing

The company baron is constantly aware of and concerned about
change. His approaches to controlling and co-ordinating, rewarding and motivating, are his approaches to influencing and
changing. The company baron will work within the current
system, even if it involves lengthy decision-making processes;
stimulate people to accept responsibilities because of their
loyalty to him and the organisation and use patronage and
personal favour as rewards. The company baron champions
phased change, step-by-step development.

In his attempts to control the rate of change, the baron is
faced with the problem of cognitive dissonance, i.e. great
personal discomfort. Trying to maintain tradition and precedence, trying to work with others, trying to keep the number
of changes taking place under control and trying to limit the
generation of too many innovative ideas can so easily lead the
company baron to feeling that the situation is out of hand. Too
many things are happening at once. The company baron's
response is: stick only to those things that we are good at.

For this reason, the company baron will adopt a two-fold
approach to influencing others: caution and increased personal
power. Caution is vital. Changing the reward and role structure
of an organisation has to be achieved in such a way that people
continue to work for the organisation and not its downfall. For
this reason, the company baron will check people's opinions
before making his play and accept that in order for people to
approve of change, lengthy decision-making processes are
inevitable.

Increased personal power is also necessary. It is one thing to
introduce change into a department or division; it is something
else to achieve one's objective through the change process. A
number of people will identify with the change process and wish
to implement their objectives. To ensure that one's own
programme of change is being achieved, one must be influential

in the organisation. Hence, the two-pronged approach of creating informal network groups to lobby in support of one's policies, and maintaining distance from subordinates and others less well known, so as to ensure that they achieve their tasks, but do not interfere with policy development.

A company baron in telecommunications

A multinational British telecommunications company was facing the prospect of having to introduce large-scale changes into the organisation. Fluctuations in world markets and increasing competition from the Japanese and Americans was forcing the company to consider a strategy of rationalisation. The managing director of the company was reluctant to introduce too many changes, too quickly. He was most reluctant to make long-serving, loyal staff, redundant.

A number of consultants were hired to examine the company. One consultant stated that not only did the company not have a well-developed marketing strategy; it did not have a well-organised marketing function. The marketing function was decentralised across a number of separate departments, which, in turn, did not operate a co-ordinated marketing strategy.

The managing director knew that poor marketing had been a weakness in the company for some time. He told the consultant that he did not wish to create a separate marketing department as it could cause too much upset in the company and an unacceptable number of staff could be made redundant. Instead, the MD has introduced a policy of phased change, whereby through early retirement and job transfer/rotation schemes, certain departments have made 'room' for re-organisation.

By co-ordinating the activities of others and with their approval, the MD had developed an acceptable longer-term strategy of change. Despite the recession, the company made a larger than expected profit in 1982.

THE VISIONARY

Approaches to controlling and co-ordinating

Although the company baron and the visionary equally work to longer-term perspectives, the visionary demands quicker results. He champions rapid change. His preference, therefore, is to adopt a strategy of direct control as opposed to co-ordination.

The visionary will attempt to lure talented experts as his lieutenants. Their function would be to put into practice his ideas. Co-ordinating with immediate subordinates will be minimal. Obviously, a certain number of meetings will have to be held so that the intentions of the visionary can be made clear. Equally, he will have to be kept up-to-date with developments in the organisation. Once it is established what needs to be done, it is expected that subordinates attempt to put his wishes into practice.

As part of the process of implementation, the visionary can tolerate confrontation and conflict from both outsiders and his

---

Developing an MBA

MBA stands for Master of Business Administration. It is a postgraduate business qualification, awarded by the more prestigious business schools to the more successful managers who have decided to take time off from full-time employment in order to develop themselves further as managers.

At one world-famous business school, which already runs a successful full-time MBA programme, it was decided to introduce a part-time MBA programme, so that successful managers could study further without interrupting their careers. Most staff in the school considered that the full-time programme required attention and modification but that they did not need a part-time programme.

Two directors were appointed, one to the full-time, the other to the part-time MBA. Both went about their new responsibilities with enthusiasm. The full-time director held formal meetings, talking to the necessary and interested faculty staff, sent memos informing the school of developments and made formal presentations to interested parties bringing them up-to-date with new ideas and developments. The full-time director, conscious of his role and position in the school, stated that on all matters concerning the full-time MBA, he should keep the school informed.

The part-time director operated in a different way. He took no notice of committees or established procedures. Anyone he wanted to see, he saw informally, often by just stopping them in the corridor. He held few meetings on how the programme should be structured, packaged and marketed. In fact, he rejected most of the advice he was offered. He did not send memos or hold meetings informing people of developments. He put into practice his ideas.

The part-time director faced criticism, that although friendly and approachable as an individual, he was wasting his time, for such a programme would not attract sufficient response from the market place. Further, colleagues became a little anxious about his buccaneering style.

As it turned out, both programmes were an outstanding success. Student numbers increased dramatically; the school made a substantial profit from the additional fees. Both directors are now held in high esteem by their colleagues.

subordinates. If others feel that a particular policy requires re-examination, is too difficult to achieve or that opposition to change could be too great, and even if an argument ensues, the visionary can well cope with the situation. In fact, greater respect is given to subordinates who confront him as long as the ultimate intention is the successful application of the visionary's basic policies.

Direct control over others is strongly applied when others oppose his policies on ethical as opposed to practical grounds and when subordinates find it difficult to make the policies work. In both cases, the visionary will attempt to remove people from their positions and, preferably, out of the organisation.

The visionary is no respecter of the system. If things are not working out, either someone is to blame or the system needs changing. Usually both. Direct intervention and taking control of the situation are common with the visionary.

In the boxed case study on p. 54 ('Developing an MBA') the director of the full-time programme behaved more as a company baron. He interacted with others on a formal basis, controlling activities and ensuring that his status or position as director was not threatened or diminished. He was effective and successful.

The part-time director behaved more as a visionary. He did not attempt to take part in the formal system. He liaised with those he considered could make a useful contribution; put his own ideas into practice and cared little about his position or whether his status increased or decreased in the eyes of others. He was effective and successful.

Perhaps the person who appointed them possessed the greatest insight. The full-time director had to make what existed work better. The part-time director had to create something new.

Approaches to rewarding and motivating

The visionary rewards those who perform competently and exhibit high energy at work. Individuals who, at the tactical level, introduce new processes or systems, alter the current structure, take calculated risks and are seen to be able to accept ever-increasing responsibilities, are likely to be offered substantial rewards. An individual who shows he has better ideas than colleagues, can accept personal criticism from peers and superiors and is capable of making the tougher decisions, such as demoting friends, is more likely to be offered money and status.

The visionary is attracted to people who exhibit high task skills and a professional approach to work. Valuing highly the skills to accomplish and complete complex tasks and not emphasising loyalties to people has a number of implications. The simple fact that an individual is invited to join a problem-solving team is sufficient reward and motivation in itself. It indicates that like-minded peers recognise the potential contribution of the individual. Whether that individual survives in that team is another matter.

However, the visionary will not forgive people if they commit one or both of the two cardinal sins: failure and proving to be a direct threat to his policies. The visionary will have little patience with so-called losers. He may even blame himself as a poor judge of character for having trusted the individual concerned.

Equally, the individual's previous accomplishments and current skills are not taken into consideration if the policies of the visionary are challenged. People either fit with the visionary or they do not. If they do not, it is far simpler to get rid of them, even if it means paying them off to get rid of them.

Unlike the company baron, the visionary does not adopt the system of patronage. For any good work done, people are either rewarded by money or position. Once the reward has been offered, the visionary no longer feels himself indebted to the individual. Non-visionaries will find themselves in the position

---

A visionary in the book trade

A fast-growing publishing company almost went bankrupt after its chairman had decided to buy another smaller publishing company. He did not consult with colleagues, nor fully explore the financial state of the company he bought. To his and his fellow directors' horror, the newly bought company had debts that wiped out the parent company's profits and further forced it to undertake a burdensome bank loan.

In order to survive, the parent company had to cut all costs and hope that working on a bare minimum budget and together with all profits made, the deficits in terms of bank loans and debts would be met. The chairman accepted some criticism for his purchase, but then firmly stated that all directors and employees would have to make sacrifices to survive. Some of the editors argued that their area of concern in the company would be adversely affected through the irresponsible actions of one man. Some of the editors took little notice of his cutback measures. Although extremely competent at their jobs and friends of the chairman, they were informed, 'accept what I tell you or get out'.

of constantly having to prove themselves to the visionary. It is unlikely that displays of friendliness, warmth and empathy will improve their position with him. The visionary expects neither himself nor others to live on past credits.

In the boxed case study on p. 56 ('A visionary in the book trade') the chairman behaved as a visionary. He only involved himself on big projects, made quick decisions and became bored with details. He expected people to make any project operate effectively once he had made the decision that time and money should be invested in that project. Equally, he disliked criticism of his policy decisions, and as in the case above, even when he was shown to have made a blunder.

Approaches to influencing and changing

The visionary depends on his skills of confrontation, direct control and personal charisma to lead others in the direction he wants. Hence, his approach to controlling and co-ordinating and rewarding and motivating are similar to his approach to influencing and changing.

Unlike the company baron, the visionary is not prone to cognitive dissonance. In fact, the bigger the change, the more unstructured the situation, the greater the risks, the more attractive is the challenge. The only discomfort he is likely to experience is when change is too slow, when tasks involve too much detail and routine and when people demand he shares out ideas and information.

If the changes at hand require improvement to the products or services offered by the organisation, then roles, rules and regulations take second place. The visionary would gather round him individuals who would enjoy a new challenge, require little or no direction as to how they should act and be able to face the responsibility that if performance (their own, their subordinates' or colleagues') was not up to standard, they would be held accountable. People considered negative or a block to further growth could be removed from their position or even have their total group or department disbanded, despite a history of competent performance. When change is required, visionaries pay little respect to people's roles, authority, standing or status in the organisation.

When a visionary is severely constrained by vested interests of groups or individuals, he may stimulate artificial crises in order to disrupt and confuse those that oppose him. Under such circumstances, both friends and enemies may be pushed aside and out of the organisation in order to start afresh. Anyone who identifies with the values of the past may be considered a block to progress.

In extreme circumstances, the visionary becomes the 'hit man' brought in to introduce rapid change when the organisation's very survival is in question.

Cubic action man

The recent appointment of Neil Shaw as the group managing director of Tate and Lyle was an important step towards climbing out of trouble for the cane sugar refinery company, famous for its sugar cubes. Shaw master-minded the closure of the company's Liverpool refinery; the shut down of the group's glucose and starch making operations at a cost of £22m and in order to help pay for such high closure costs, he sold the company's fleet of three ships for £11m. During the period of rapid change, he fought off one take-over bid. Despite an uncertain future and further reconstruction and rationalisation, Shaw seems to have gained the respect of his colleagues. The first half profits for 1981 stood at £12.3m, 30% higher than the previous comparable period. Further closures, redundancies and new developments are to take place. Tate and Lyle has changed from a passive to a more proactive, even predator organisation. If Shaw has his way, T & L could further diversify into the plastics and leisure fields.

(Source: Financial Times Monday, Sept.7, 1981, p.9)

Shaw seems to have behaved as a visionary. He appreciates strategy and seems to be able to stand apart from his current situation and put into practice remedial measures, which may not be to everyone's liking. He has exhibited the ability to disengage from previous values, from the influence of his friends and colleagues and introduce his vision of how things ought to be. How long visionaries are allowed to remain as visionaries and not adopt the organisational position of the company baron, is a debatable point.

EMERGENCE OF TYPE

Most people recognise that different types of people exist. Most people further recognise that simply in order to function, they have to interact with people they like and dislike; with people with whom they do and do not sympathise. The perception/ action model (Chapter 1) provides a framework by which to 'map out' and understand the people we meet in our world. Yet, people do not just stay in their own little world. They try to expand; they try to influence others according to their own values. In other words, they attempt to make the world of others comparable with their own.

In order to understand which of the organisational politicians is gaining the upper hand in today's organisations, it is necessary to examine the pressures or forces that are shaping our organisations. Is one or more particular type of politician emerging who in turn shapes our organisations in particular ways, thereby forming a typical organisation culture? These issues are explored in Part II.

Part Two
ORGANISATIONAL PRESSURES

Assessing the situation

Frederikson: Look, I am within an inch of getting the K.Y. contract. The very thought of having to ask Dawson and his group and that idiot who was on my interviewing panel makes me want to give up with this K.Y. thing!

New junior executive: What else can we do? The chairman has stated he wants greater inter-departmental co-operation.

Frederikson: Yeh, but what about my image? I'll look such an idiot if K.Y. find those two screwballs on the team.

Thinks for a while then says: O.K.! Here's what to do. You contact K.Y.'s computer guy. Ask him to present his case at the meeting in such a way that he alone can handle the data input. Tell him we prefer him on the team as he's so damn good and we will tell K.Y.'s chairman that as well.

For me, I am getting in touch with their contracts guy to see if some lousy little job can be found for Dawson and his group.

Junior executive: You know, this could mean Dawson being demoted from divisional executive to plant manager. His department is already in the red. Could also lose some of his people!

Frederikson: Couldn't have happened to a nicer guy!

Moral

So you want to do your own thing? O.K. Then work the system before the system works you.

3 Dependency or Innovation

Every organisation has something special about it which gives it a unique identity. Enter into any organisation and you will find that they have their own ways of doing things. They have their own formal systems, their own patterns of informal interactions and their own particular views on work and approaches to conducting work relationships.

Dig a little deeper into that organisation and a number of different factors begin to emerge. Particular divisions, departments or groups have developed their own self-image. These self-images are partly formed by the people present in that situation. However, there are certain self-images or characteristics that survive long after the people active in the situation have left. Possibly one of the greatest rivalries in today's organisations has been and is between marketing and production departments. Once one of the old heads of department leaves and the new man attempts reconciliation, he is likely to be opposed by his own side and the other.

Hence, any organisation has a number of factors operating simultaneously. Anyone who wishes to survive and progress within the organisation has to learn the rules of a number of games.

Management academics have termed such phenomena organisation culture or organisation climate. Why have particular identities or cultures or climates emerged? To answer this question, four themes are presented which have led to the development of particular identities or cultures in our organisations. The themes are:

1 Small *v* large: was size ever a choice?
2 Outer *v* inner-directed.

3 Skills *v* insight.
4 Office politics: the culture of intolerance.

The question is, which of the four politicians fit best in today's organisations?

SMALL *v* LARGE: WAS SIZE EVER A CHOICE?

Probably the most important phenomenon in today's organisation is size. The most powerful and influential of organisations in any nation state, whether in the public or private sector, are large. These organisations employ many people. They buy and sell extensive areas of property. They offer a wide range of different products or services. Decisions made on whether to expand and enter into new markets, or to contract and conserve funds, affect a number of smaller businesses or even whole communities.

On becoming big

In Europe, the UK and the USA, the time of the great mergers, takeovers and strivings to become big took place from the 1950s onwards. No one has been exempt from the effects of organisation growth.

In the USA, the motor industry is dominated by the big three: General Motors, Ford and Chrysler. The big three would have dominated the UK and Europe had it not been for attempts by Peugeot and Renault to penetrate the American market.

In the banking world, the great UK bank mergers of the 1960s brought into operation the big four banks. In the food and drinks industry, great mergers such as Cadbury's and Schweppes have produced huge multinational organisations striving to capture world markets.

Insurance broking is no longer a small personalised service. All the main brokers have transatlantic links. The UK broker Hogg Robinson, for example, owns 30 per cent of the Markel Corp., a small US broker. In addition, Hogg Robinson has entered into partnership with a subsidiary of Republic Steel of the USA to form Republic Hogg Robinson.

The public services in the UK also underwent thoroughgoing changes. Between 1966 and 1974, nursing, social work and social services, local government and the health services in general, were all reorganised into larger structures. The reason for such changes was admirable: to form administrative units which could meet the demands of comparable population sizes. It was felt that previously, an unequal distribution of social welfare and health resources was in practice. Yet, all the programmes for change in the public services had one striking similarity: the emphasis on administrative rationality accompanied by a seemingly sub-conscious belief that simply reforming internal management structures would eventually lead to improvements in the health, care and satisfaction of the public at large.

The critics and their criticisms

Some have argued that no matter how well a large organisation is managed, bigness in itself prevents effectiveness in terms of quantity and quality of work output and in terms of job satisfaction.

Schumacher (1974), of 'small is beautiful' fame, stated that the only real alternative to bigness is smallness. In smaller units, people talk to each other, know each other and can use their inventiveness and intuition to think of new and exciting ideas, both for the benefit of the group and the organisation as a whole.

Professor Reg Revans (1976) the world-respected promotor of 'action learning', backs Schumacher by indicating that when people feel they can no longer talk to each other, then organisations are faced with insurmountable problems. Numerous others provide research data that small units offer ideal working conditions and more efficient use of resources.[*]

The theme of the critics of large organisations is that with increases in size, control, co-ordination and maintaining direction become virtually impossible to practise. Management need to have good control over what is happening in an organisation, simply to achieve efficient operations. Yet the larger an organisation becomes, the more difficult is effective control. How can any one individual or small group at the top totally digest what is happening in their organisation?

As a consequence, senior and middle level management may become too concerned with maintaining their own position and status and may react by over-controlling the activities of others.

---

[*] See selective bibliography for Chapter 3, pp. 165-6.

In situations of over-control, creativity and initiative are dampened. People become unable or unwilling to generate new ideas or even pass information up and down the hierarchical line. Disagreements, arguments, rifts and splits can become a normal part of everyday work life. Maintaining one's distance from one's own fellow men could become more important than working together to achieve something.

More enlightened management may realise that effective control is being lost. They may try to cope with the situation by decentralising, in effect giving sub-units in the organisation more autonomy.

On the one hand, decentralisation may reduce over-control, and give people the opportunity to promote their innovative ideas.

On the other hand, with increasing sub-unit autonomy comes a greater need for co-ordination. There is always the danger that co-ordination of sub-units becomes impossible. The sub-units in large organisations could engage in activities that are out of the control and co-ordinative power of those at the top. The result is that people find themselves stressed, have poor relationships with colleagues, superiors and subordinates, do not know why they are doing certain tasks and feel that ambiguous demands are being made on them.

If control and co-ordination become impossible for any one man or set of men at the top, not because they are incompetent but rather because events and conditions are too complex for anyone to comprehend totally and act upon quickly, then how is it possible to achieve strategic objectives and maintain clarity of direction?

It must be no surprise to the more aware senior manager in any large organisation to find that his subordinates do not know whether they are still going in the right direction. Further, they may not know what direction they were supposed to go in the first place.

Under such conditions, the visionaries would not be valued. They would probably be considered a threat. Their ideas and energy could lead to even greater splits and divisions which would require further control.

Why bigness?

If control, co-ordination and maintaining direction become

problematic with increases in size; if relationships and formal
rules and procedures become more and more complex with
growth and expansion, why choose that the organisation should
grow? In fact, was size ever a conscious choice?

Probably not. let us postulate that growth occurred and
people did not really choose it. There are four reasons for such
an assumption.

1 The philosophy that management adopt is that the
development of the organisation and its growth in size are
synonymous. If an organisation is doing well, has
penetrated new markets and provides additional services,
the assumption in practice is do what you did before plus
what you want to do now – therefore become bigger!

2 Combined with a need to grow and do well comes anxiety.
Most organisations that have grown have also done well in
the past. They may have acquired a considerable market
share for their products and want to continue their success
by improving their position in the market. The anxieties
arise from the feeling, *what would happen if we do not
expand?* The alternative may be to let other organisations
jump in and capture a market nurtured by us. Success
brings with it a question that most cannot answer, *if we do
not continue to grow what else do we do?*

3 Economies of scale. By growing bigger, it is possible to
establish greater control over productivity, resources and
investments. Large investments can be concentrated on
one location, allowing for little wastage and hardly any
duplication of resources. The argument goes that by
becoming bigger, one can reduce the level of excessive
overheads. The argument is plausible.

4 Optimism. With reorganisation, changes of career
structure and changes in the reward system, most people
feel optimistic. New jobs are there for the taking, improved
working conditions and rewards are available and the
general hustle and bustle of growth and new opportunities
give rise to feelings of a prosperous future. Things must be
good if all this is happening. Whatever doubts people had
are washed away in a torrent of exploration and participation, in a culture of working together towards the new
goals. The lone, doubting voice questioning such a rosy
view of the future is neither respected nor liked.

British Leyland – by an OD consultant

Ray Charlton, an internal organisation development (OD) consultant with British Leyland (BL) recently wrote (1982) about the developments in the company that have led to its present crisis position.

For BL, three major phases of company organisation can be identified.

The first phase (1968–74), which followed the merger of British Motor Holdings Limited and Leyland Motor Corp. Ltd, was one of anticipated expansion and great hope for the future. The newly formed conglomerate hoped to expand its production and sales to compete with the biggest and the best. New management systems and practices were introduced and a large number of specialists, some outside the motor industry, were recruited, all bringing with them new ideas and techniques.

In the second phase (1974–78), the first period was seen as a false dawn. By the end of 1974, the company approached the government for funds. Funding was granted but only after further re-organisation. Previous car company divisions were merged into a large centralised line and staff structure. In addition, there was a reshuffling of management personnel and the major functions and reporting lines were re-shaped.

In the third phase (from 1978 onwards), BL was placed under the leadership of Michael Edwards. Further re-organisation and rationalisation took place, whereby inessential activities were relentlessly discarded in an effort to keep the corporate head above water. The new survival order was either do the job or get out. That situation still holds.

For Ray Charlton, a number of reasons exist for BL's demise.

Size. The company became too big too quickly.

Integration. As the company grew, there were few attempts to bring together the various parts of the company under some form of corporate philosophy.

Over-optimism on the part of management. Simply because the company had grown in size did not mean it would be successful.

The lack of strategic thinking and integration on the part of the internal OD consultants meant that there was no co-ordinated effort by the very people who were employed to provide consultancy and training to meet the company's needs.

As line management found it difficult to cope with size, so to did the OD consultants.

There are a few questions that Ray Charlton did not discuss but that I should raise. Did most managers really want change? Did management really want integration? What were, and are, the predominant beliefs and values of management in BL? Could it be that the company was dominated by traditionalists and company barons, which would have made any real change and development almost impossible?

On being big: on being human

What happens in large organisations?

Probably Schumacher, Revans and all the other critics of big institutions are right. People find it difficult to appreciate the totality of a large organisation. They lose their sense of direction. They may not even understand why senior management attempts to control and co-ordinate their activities. In turn, senior management may be viewed as insensitive, interfering and out of date. In fact, why should people bother to try to gain a 'birds-eye' view of the total organisation and what it is trying to achieve? Over 95 per cent of people employed by organisations have no financial share in the organisation. Why struggle with the strategic problems of the organisation? After all, that is what senior management are paid to do.

The career hierarchy is a further constraint on people developing an appreciation of the total business. The structured pattern of jobs and roles, whereby each individual needs only to understand what he has to do in order to get his job done, provides for limited vision. Each person does not need to know about the overall organisation. All that needs to be shown is competent performance in one's present job and sufficient potential for the next position higher up.

In situations where people are not required to understand fully what is happening around them, then the values of the traditionalist come to predominate. People only identify with those they actually meet. Over a period of time, groups of people emerge who champion only their distinct self-image, sometimes to the detriment of all else. After a while people go to great lengths to ensure that they are different from other groups in the organisation, even at the cost of quality or quantity of production.

It is a strange phenomenon that as organisations have become larger, people not only seek out their particular group to form a separate culture, but further take pride in ensuring they do not understand the true nature of their organisation. Problems are shunted backwards and forwards, between individuals, groups and departments. Skills at passing the buck rather than the skills of problem solving are the desired attributes a manager should develop. *Let someone else worry about that* must be a phrase commonly spoken and hangs in the corridors of most organisations.

In such circumstances, the company baron will excel. The traditionalists need him to guide and direct their activities. They may not like him, but they know he will resist radical change and provide support and a sense of security. The company baron will at least stabilise the situation and create some semblance of order.

OUTER v INNER DIRECTED

We have already discussed outer and inner-directedness in Chapter 1. Let us explore it further.

Table 3.1
Attitudes and behaviours

Outer-directed	Inner-directed
Role-oriented	Self-oriented
Status-conscious	Personal goals-oriented
Checks with others before doing something	Does what individual thinks is required
Highest rewards are improving one's position	Highest reward is recognition for competent task performance
Unlikely to introduce dramatic change	Will introduce changes that are considered necessary
Will take leadership if others give support	Will take leadership to satisfy personal drive

Table 3.1 lists certain outer- and inner-directed attitudes and behaviours.

Outer-directed people are more role-oriented, status-conscious, will dislike introducing sudden, dramatic or unpopular changes and will aim to take the lead only if others provide full support.

Inner-directed people decide what they wish to do and do it.

They are concerned with the standard of results of their endeavours and if need be, introduce unpopular changes and accept leadership responsibilities without the full support of their peers.

Does size of organisation influence whether people become predominantly more outer- than inner-directed? – yes!

As stated, the larger an organisation becomes, the more difficult it is to practise effective control and co-ordination. The career hierarchy provides a way out of these difficulties. People are both controlled and co-ordinated because they wish to be. Anyone who wishes to follow a career in an organisation must first appreciate the existing career structure. Then he will know what is required of him in his present job and also what he would have to do in order to gain promotion and thereby improve his status and financial standing. However, the man does not determine his own actions to attain promotion – the system does. It is simply not necessary to exhibit competence beyond the requirements of the role or job. All that is necessary is do what is required. From there on, people identify with outer-directedness. They become more concerned with what someone else thinks rather than what they think themselves.

From the individual's point of view, it is all too easy to become more concerned with promotion and doing what is required. From the moment an individual is offered a job, the pressure is on to improve performance with the manager or the supervisor determining both the quality and quantity of output. If performance is improved, then the two key rewards available are more money or promotion. In reality promotion means upward mobility and very soon the person is in turn managing others and not directly applying his own professional expertise. The ones who fit the system go up. The others are left behind to do the work.

It is the company baron who fits and goes up.

Some people's actions, thoughts and feelings are almost exclusively determined by what their manager thinks of them, and how long it will take them to be promoted.

Promotions, company barons and the police

One of the issues that has attracted substantial attention and debate amongst policemen in the Metropolitan Police (London) has been their annual qualification review (AQR) system. This is the annual review that each policeman has with a superior concerning his present job performance and future potential. Like other formal review systems, the AQR is based on a complex form to be completed by a superior on a subordinate, examining in detail not only present job performance but various leadership qualities and potential for higher rank.

The subordinate reads most of the report except for one section which is a confidential statement by the supervisor on the subordinate. The report is then checked by a higher ranking police officer to see whether the supervisor has made an accurate assessment.

Despite various checks and balances, the AQR continues to be the centre of controversy. Some feel parts of the AQR form are too complex. Others feel it is too simple. Many feel that there is insufficient training on the use of the form and hence many supervisors are viewed as providing an inaccurate picture of their subordinates.

The degree of anxiety and attention the AQR receives is understandable. Other than for the ranks of Sergeant and Inspector where candidates have to pass formal examinations to be promoted, no candidate ever applies for promotion to the next rank. A superior officer will place one or more candidates before an interview board who will consider his/her promotion to the next rank. Hence, the view a superior has of his subordinates and the information he can call upon to back up his view, are absolutely vital considerations for ambitious subordinates.

One policeman stated, 'Knowing how to ask for permission to do something is more important than doing it'.

That policeman was smart. He sensed that company barons love the patronage game.

SKILLS v INSIGHT

Large organisations need well-qualified employees for two reasons.

First, the organisation needs the specialists to produce, market and sell its products or services. Numerous specialist skills are required in that process: specialists who design the products; people trained to make the products; marketing specialists who develop strategies to sell the products; salesmen who actually sell the goods; administrators and accountants who examine the viability of the organisation and its ventures; and human resource specialists whose aim is to develop the quality of working life so that those producing and selling the goods are sufficiently motivated to continue doing so.

Second, in order to give a career hierarchy credibility in the eyes of the organisation's employees, it is necessary to introduce standards of competence. In this way, the best are supposedly selected on the basis of their achievements and competence. An effective measure of high competence is qualifications. Qualifications, however, are controlled by certain professional societies. Many of the professional societies wield sufficient influence to ensure that people without their qualifications are unlikely to be promoted no matter how well they perform on the job.

One should not underestimate the influence of the profession upon its members and employing organisations. Consider the factors that determine professionalism.

The issue of control of persons acting in a professional capacity and of the tasks they can and cannot perform is most important. As can be seen from Table 3.2, control over professional persons is expressed in three different ways: knowledge that is exclusive to relatively few people; recognition from key members of the community that a particular group provides a unique service; controlling procedures identified and enforced by the professional body, setting down appropriate standards of service.

Table 3.2
Factors determining professionalism

Control	Moral Identity	Time
Knowledge exclusive to a few people	Persons of similar values putting their views into practice	Certain groups who withstand criticism and remain intact over long periods of time are likely to become established as a profession
Communal recognition in the sense of standing distinctly apart from other groups in employment		Once established, the group develops a commonly recognised professional identity
Prescribed standards of service over task activities and interpersonal relationships		

Moral identity is a strong influence on the behaviour of people. By entering a profession, people of compatible personal values can put into practice their view of how things ought to be.

Survival over long periods of time is crucial. Groups that describe their activities as professional and remain intact over long periods of time are eventually recognised by the community at large, as providing some sort of professional service. Apart from groups such as doctors and lawyers, where little disagreement exists as to their professional status, a number of occupations (e.g. estate agents, marketing and personnel managers) are now generally recognised as having some sort of professional status. The growth and development of marketing and personnel managers has involved a struggle over a number of years in order to gain professional status.

The net effect is that two strong influences on how to behave appropriately at work are simultaneously in operation: the influence of the profession and the influence of the organisation.

Ironically, professional bodies and large organisations are similar; they propound traditional values and precedence. Both wish to control their membership in terms of who they accept and once in, how these people should think and feel. To do something that ventures outside the guidelines or rules laid down could mean a reprimand, or, in extreme cases, expulsion from the society or organisation. Introducing changes could be a long, tedious and often unrewarding process. After all, one is up against the society's company barons.

Becoming qualified and becoming professional improves an individual's status and job mobility. It does not, however, improve his capacity to be creative and introduce fresh and new ideas. The process of attaining a formal skill may even dampen the potential creative insights of the person. People are professionally trained in both how to do things and how to think and feel. What sort of creativity is that?

Chief executives on chief executives

Professor Charles Margerison of Cranfield School of Management conducted a study (1980) examining how chief executives succeed. The study was conducted in the UK and his sample was the *Times* top 1,000 companies and their chief executives.

Margerison asked the chief executives to list those factors that they considered most important in their rise to the top. Overall, 18 factors were identified (Table 3.3).

Factor number 18, the least important influence, is, 'having special off-the-job management training.' Still low on the list of priorities is factor number 14, 'having sound technical training.'

Only a few chief executives in interviews stated that technical or even management training would be an advantage. For them, training can make a person blinkered; they develop too narrow a view. For a chief executive to be effective, he must have an overall view of the company and good appreciation of market trends. The last thing a chief executive would want is to act as a technical or professional specialist.

Table 3.3
What factors have helped you develop as a manager?

Rank Order	Statements	Score out of 100
1	Ability to work with a wide variety of people	78.4
2	Early overall responsibility for important tasks	74.8
3	A need to achieve results	74.8
4	Leadership experience early in career	73.6
5	Wide experience in many functions before age 35	67.6
6	An ability to do deals and negotiate	66.4
7	Willingness to take risks	62.8
8	Having more ideas than other colleagues	61.6
9	Being stretched by immediate bosses	60.4
10	An ability to change managerial style to suit occasion	58.8
11	A desire to seek new opportunities	56.8
12	Being visible to top management before age 30	56.0
13	Family support (wife/parent)	55.2
14	Having sound technical training	54.8
15	Having a manager early in your career who acted as a model (from whom you learned a lot)	52.0
16	Overseas managerial/work experience	41.2
17	Experience of leadership in armed forces (peace-time/wartime)	40.4
18	Having special 'off-the-job' management training	32.8

Scale of importance

1	20	40	60	80	100

| Low | Fair | Average | Substantial | Great |

Office politics: the culture of intolerance

Office politics are nothing more than the interactions and relationships people have with each other in their office, department, group or unit. A feature of office politics is that interactions are conducted in relatively small, compartmentalised, somewhat isolated groups. The groups may be in close physical proximity to each other in the organisation. One group may be just across the corridor to other groups. Yet the isolation is self-created.

Another aspect of office politics is that they can be an unpleasant experience. They come into play because people feel unable to question organisational norms. Office politics are as much the result of a loss of self-direction than anything else. The organisation determines whom you meet by telling you where to work. The organisation indicates what you are through the roles it gives you.

The issues of office politics are those of the small group. The wider world is too amorphous to bear serious consideration. People chatter about each other; what they did today and yesterday. Status is important. Whether people are paying attention to the pecking order is a more important feature of organisational life than what we do in the future. Product innovation and new developments are given less attention than people's titles and forms of formal address.

Not hurting the feelings of the company baron

Recently, a senior manager in a well-known international bank for whom I had provided consultancy services for a number of years, called a meeting to discuss an important and expensive forthcoming training programme for senior bank executives. After initial discussions of over one hour, my banking colleague indicated that he had a personal problem concerning his work.

He stated that he had recently been promoted and as a perk was entitled to a larger, more luxurious company car. However he and his boss were entitled to the same group of cars, such as Rover, Audis and expensive Ford estates. The problem was not to upset the boss's status and authority by purchasing a vehicle that could be interpreted as being bigger, better or more luxurious. What to do, for the boss had an Audi? Final choice, Ford estate. My banking colleague did not like Ford cars but considered it an expedient selection, bearing in mind his view of what his boss was really like.

Time spent on discussing the programme – 86 minutes. Time spent on discussing cars – some of the morning and most of the afternoon. Cost of programme for three-year period – £1 million

plus. Cost of car – £7,500 approximately ($14,000).
Well, at least we did not hurt the feelings of the company
baron!
Problem is, I have never quite worked out to this day whether
the real company baron was my colleague or his boss – probably
both.

It is an old story. In large organisations individuals can so
easily become dependent on the hierarchy. People generate
status differences between themselves, develop limited vision
and ambitions and desire security rather than exploration.

The unpleasant side of office politics is worth examination, as
this is how most people probably experience politics in
organisations. There are good reasons why negative feelings
arise.

First, the need for conformity. Those who promulgate the
values of their group/unit/department demand conformity
from those around them. Toe the line; stick with the group; keep
things the way they are, are the pressures brought to bear on all
individuals in the situation.

Second, conformity is achieved by controlling people's
behaviour. Most control mechanisms are socially subtle.
Tradition, custom and group norms usually ensure that the
majority of individuals behave appropriately. Should anyone be
found to resist group norms, then cruder pressures are applied.
The individual is told he cannot continue with his current
behaviours. He may be made to feel guilty in that his continued
behaviour is causing harm to friends and colleagues. Unless he
changes, he will not only hurt himself but also others. If all else
fails, then expulsion from the group is likely.

Third, innovation and originality are disliked. Anyone who
introduces new ideas naturally disrupts the status quo.
Applying new ideas involves re-examining how certain things
have been done in the past. That simple process of re-
examination could be perceived as threatening. Re-examination
and exploration are processes fraught with ambiguity. From the
traditionalist's point of view, it is unclear why people question
what is happening and where that will take them. Quite
naturally, the simplest solution is to reject the people who are
seen to generate ambiguity. Visionaries will naturally generate
ambiguity in the eyes of others, so visionaries should be kept
out.

Finally, perhaps the most important reason why office

politics have an unpleasant flavour stems from the feelings of righteousness and legitimacy that certain people have when pressurising others to conform. People with outer-directed values try to convince others with missionary zeal. Anyone who threatens that way of life has to be shown they are wrong and be removed if they do not change their attitude. It becomes impossible to communicate with anyone who is certain that rejecting you is the right and proper course of action.

The university company barons

At a well-known US business school, a young, talented and energetic faculty member made the unforgiveable mistake of doing something not traditionally practised in that department. Thereby, his colleagues eventually managed to get rid of him altogether. What did he do?

He made the inexcusable error of stating that most academic research carried out at business schools was simply a waste of time. Most research studies were of no help to businessmen and did not even address the 'real problems in the outside world.'

Folly upon folly, he repeated his view to his peers on numerous occasions. What was more, he went out to business people to see if he could help them with their problems. For such a service he charged a fee. The young faculty member used his talents well. After a while, the young man was much in demand. He was generating a substantial income outside his university salary.

Some time on, one senior professor demanded an interview with the faculty member in question.

'Look, son', said the senior professor, 'it's not that I mind you earning some extra money! It's just – what are you? A consultant or an academic?'

'I am an academic consultant. I utilise the theory and concepts in my field to help straighten out other people's business problems. What's more, all my consultancy interventions provide for my research data. I am getting far better and far richer information now than I would have, had I done more traditional research. I think I can write better articles and books this way. I tell you, our students will benefit a lot!'

'Look, there is no such thing as traditional or more modern research. Research is research – see! Second, I sure as hell like to see you try and get some of that stuff published. Most journal editors would just throw it out!' snapped the senior professor. 'What's more – you don't get tenure until you publish!'

'OK, OK, Don't worry. I'll publish', said the young man in fast retreat.

The faculty member kept his promise. He published a series of articles in reasonably respected academic journals. In the articles, he used his consultancy experiences as case examples to support certain new theories he was developing.

The time came for the senior faculty members to decide whether to offer the young man a further contract, tenure or nothing.

'Yeh, OK, so he's published', said one of the faculty appointing committee, 'but have you guys read his stuff?'

The faculty member passed round copies of articles to other faculty members.

'It's just plain weak', said one of the committee, after skimping through some pages.

'There is no real data here', said another.

'Just a series of cases. We don't even know whether they are accurately reported', said a third.

'How the hell can you develop theory when there is no substance to back it?' said the chairman of the appointing committee.

After some discussion, one member of the committee offered a different view.

'Well, he has published. He has also published more than some of us have', said the lone individual. 'What's more, some business people I have spoken to say his ideas make sense. They reckon he has got good theory'.

'What the hell are you talking about?' demanded the chairman of the committee. 'Do you want to make us the laughing stock of the academic world?'

After further discussion, it was decided that no further contract should be offered to the young faculty member. He left.

Years on, the young man, now middle-aged, exceptionally wealthy, runs two consulting businesses and has been visiting professor to a number of well-respected business schools. Two of his books are standard reading on a number of MBA programmes. Many academics consider his books to provide a valuable insight to both theory and practice.

I asked him how he now felt about his earlier experiences.

'Hell, if it hadn't been for those shits that gave me the sack, I'd still be driving some five-year-old Ford and worrying about paying my bills', he laughed in reply.

What is the message?

Where organisations are large and outer-directed values predominate, what choice do most people really have? The choice is a simple one – fit in or stay out.

To fit in, you need to accept the prevailing culture; become part of the group; make yourself visible, acceptable and non-threatening to those at the top. In other words, make a conscious effort to adjust both behavioural style and underlying attitudes so that they are acceptable. Acceptable to whom? Why, to the traditionalists and company barons. Traditionalists and company barons fit more comfortably into large-sized organisations where outer-directed values have become the norm.

To stay out usually means leaving the organisation altogether. To stay out and not to leave is to voluntarily accept misery. Whatever harm the process of fitting in or staying out does to individuals, it damages organisations even more. It generates the attitude of *Them and Us* – the subject of our next chapter.

4 Them and Us

In organisations where many cultures exist, and where outer-directedness becomes the dominant value, then splits, divisions, conflict and confrontation become common. People pay more attention to emphasising the differences between them. Over a period of time, people develop skills at erecting and maintaining barriers between themselves and others in the organisation. The organisation has finally reached the state of Them and Us.

Them and Us is a state of organisational attrition. Two or more groups of people take opposing positions and attempt to browbeat the other side to accept only their particular viewpoint. Hitting out at the other side becomes as important as, or more important than, the very survival of the organisation.

A common them and us attitude has historically developed between management and trade unions. However, it can also occur between middle management and senior management, between production department and marketing department, between personnel department and the rest of the organisation. Them and Us has for some time been an area of grave concern, for example, the Ford Motor Company.

Organisations: providers or battleground?

What are organisations – providers of goods, services and employment, or a battleground?

On 5 November 1980, Mr Paul Roots, the employee relations director of Ford Motor Co. (UK), sent a memo (the conduct code) to hourly paid employees concerning unconstitutional stoppages. The memo stated that:

1 The company faced low productivity due to stoppages of work.
2 The company and the unions had jointly developed a procedure agreement on how to handle problems that arose in the workplace without loss of production or wages.
3 Nevertheless, stoppages and strikes had continued without

referral to the procedure agreement.

4 Employees who took part in unconstitutional stoppages would be suspended without pay from the remainder of the existing shift and for the whole of the following shift unless they agreed to resume work.

5 Management would request employees not involved in the stoppage to re-man the job which has stopped. If they refused, lay-offs of employees without pay would be implemented as soon as they could no longer be gainfully employed.

It took seven months of union pressure, a strike of some 20,000 workers, reported lost production of 8,660 vehicles with a show-room value of £39m ($82m approximately) to force Ford's management to drop their conduct code.

(Source: Financial Times)

Strikes are nothing new to Ford. They have a history of management/trade union confrontation stretching over the last 20 years. Yet Ford are no better or worse off than other companies in the motor trade specifically, or in manufacturing generally. Ford, as so many other companies, are acting out their part in a ritual of bitter differences. The question is, how did the ritual arise, what does it do to people and for how long will it go on?

Why Them and Us?

There are two reasons why these attitudes come to dominate so many facets of organisational life: lack of trust, and keeping the organisation clean.

Lack of trust

Trust is synonymous with commitment. Offering commitment indicates that the person is both willing and able to do what he has pledged. When one party views the other party as unwilling or unable to honour their commitments, then they do not trust the intentions and actions of the other side. They are in a state of lack of trust. This can arise for a number of reasons, the most common being difference of status and lack of opportunity for development.

Difference of status. In organisations where being outer-directed is of greater importance than being inner-directed, acquiring higher and higher status is an important stimulus to action. Common forms of status are impressive-sounding job titles, larger offices, improved office furniture and carpeting, car, and entertainment allowance.

On the positive side, status can be conferred as recognition of a person's outstanding abilities or contribution. It does not really matter what form the status takes. What is important is that being offered increased status constitutes recognition of the contribution that someone has made and socially elevating them above their peers. For some, being offered status is a greater reward than a rise in pay. To be elevated in the eyes of both peers and superiors is the greatest form of advancement.

What of the reactions of others when this happens? If the overall feeling of the groups is that the right individual was rewarded in the most appropriate way, then it is likely that the person will be offered greater respect and have more influence over his group. Under such circumstances, the individual has a good chance of breaking down barriers between Them and Us.

However, if status rewards are offered to an individual who is considered unworthy by his group, then respect for the person is likely to fall. People may react by paying little attention to his ideas, suggestions or commands. In extreme circumstances, people may actively try to undermine him. Whenever status rewards are offered to partly or wholly undeserving individuals, the Them and Us barriers are quickly erected. The person who accepted the reward is isolated. He becomes one of Them.

Lack of opportunity for development. The situation is made worse when individuals consider either that there are few opportunities for promotion (blocked career paths) and/or the jobs they hold are dull and repetitive, with little chance of doing something exciting and new (poor quality of work life).

If people feel that their career paths are blocked, possibly because the wrong people are getting the jobs or there are no jobs to get, they will eventually consider the system they work for as unjust and in need of dramatic change. In order to change the system, those who manage it have to be removed from their position. After a while, both sides fail to appreciate the intentions and contribution of the other. The only forms of meaningful communication seem to be conflict and confrontation. The only way to get anything done is to show the other side who is boss.

British manufacturing has suffered from a shopfloor/ management Them and Us attitude for decades. Shopfloor personnel find it difficult to identify with the aspirations, actions and objectives of management. From the shopfloor operative's point of view, he has for so long been denied the right to compete for management positions, that he would now not have one were it offered. From the manager's side, he has to cope with the frustration and uncertainty of not knowing whether production will continue and whether deadlines with customers will be met. The chief executive of a medium-sized engineering company in Manchester stated:

> If this year, we win big contracts and make money, the unions will want more money in terms of productivity agreements. If next year we lose some contracts, the unions will still want the same money and I won't be able to pay it. Why bother making more and more money?

To a certain extent, the situation is out of the manager's control. He cannot promote everybody; he cannot even promote 50 per cent. The managerial positions are simply not there. However, top management can attempt to improve the culture of their workplace, bringing the operatives into the decision-making process by trying to find different ways of improving their quality of working life. The objective is to turn traditionalists into team coaches.

Turning traditionalists into team coaches – the American experience

Despite the many differences among the various occupational groups in the US private and public sectors, there has been a dramatic decline in trade union membership. In 1973, total trade union membership was approximately 28 per cent of people in employment. The latest estimate for 1982 is around 18 per cent.

Such a development has to be seen against a background of management/trade union/shopfloor co-operation on quality of work life programmes (QWL). The American approach to industrial democracy is to focus on direct participation, i.e. actually improving the quality of one's working life. One of the successful QWL projects took place at the General Motors Plant at Tarrytown, New York.

The plant manager at Tarrytown made the initial approach to the union stating his concern over high absenteeism, low efficiency, poor management/shopfloor relations and poor quality control. In co-operation with the unions, a QWL programme was put into practice, emphasising product quality control. A pilot project was launched in the glass production area because of the mix of people – blacks, whites, Portuguese, Cubans, Puerto Ricans, both males and females – and because of that particular area's poor quality of performance.

This group's attitude was one of resentment towards both union and management. Efficiency was low due primarily to water leaks and glass breakage. There were 36 workers in the group, 18 on days and 18 on nights. An advisory committee was set up, several members chosen by the workers themselves, together with an elected union representative. The management added three superintendents and two foremen to the committee which would meet once each week or more often if requested to check on the group, review problems and discuss how to resolve them. The workers were able to speak up and had as much influence in the group as the managers. Then a follow-up would take place to see that whatever was agreed would be implemented.

About six months after the programme started (throughout, the emphasis had been on problem solving and worker participation in discussing and deciding improvements in their job and their departments), the group reported that glass breakage had almost been eliminated, and that water leaks had just about disappeared.

They had saved the company over $26,000 in glass breakage and over $60,000 in stopping water leaks. The quality had improved and the efficiency of the group was restored. The group was no longer being disciplined by the management. Morale improved and absenteeism had dropped from 12 per cent to less than 3 per cent. Attitudes towards management and towards union representatives had also improved.

Workers from other departments began asking for a QWL programme. In the chassis department and the soft trim department, with over 700 workers, 98.9 per cent of the workforce volunteered to be in the programme. And so it went on, involving more of the workforce and getting similar results.

Ultimately, 95 per cent of the plant's 3,800 employees were included in a QWL programme at a cost to General Motors of $1.5 million. The strategy turned Tarrytown into the company's most efficient assembly facility.

Source: John Bank (1982).

The Tarrytown experiment clearly indicates that it is possible to transform an organisation dominated by financial losses, strife, lack of identity with the company, lack of self-responsibility, and poor quality workmanship into one where pride in one's work, improved management/union relations, and the production of high quality goods all become the norm. Essentially the transformation is from outer-directed values to inner-directed values – from being traditionalists to becoming team coaches. In order to improve management/union relationships and the quality of finished products, it is necessary to improve (and always continue improving) the degree of challenge and self-responsibility at work. If people are given the opportunity to express themselves at work, then not only are the finished products likely to be of a higher quality and in greater quantity, but the trust between those who manage and those who produce may improve.

When the company barons lose control. I recently interviewed one of the management staff who had experienced the strikes of 1979–80 at the Linwood plant, formerly owned by Chrysler Motors, situated just outside Glasgow, Scotland. This is his story.

Linwood: the inside story

One of the senior managers stated that all problems at Linwood stemmed from management's mismanagement. The barriers between management and the shopfloor were becoming greater and more insurmountable day by day.

In an effort to challenge and attempt to break trade union power, management stated that unless certain agreed and established procedures and productivity agreements were practised by the shopfloor, cuts in take-home pay and redundancies would result. However, management bowed out. They did not carry out their threats when challenged by the shopfloor stewards.

The workforce did not have any particular loyalties to either side. However, when they repeatedly saw management giving way, they assumed that the shop stewards must have a good case. In practice, discipline and productivity dropped. Agreements were not being implemented due to management's mismanagement. The Company Barons had lost control.

New managers were brought into Linwood and they argued that all agreements between management and trade unions should be upheld. Having won the support of the established managers, the new managers confronted the shop stewards. The shop stewards organised strikes. Some of the strikes were long and bitter affairs. Eventually, they petered out because management did not back down. After a time, absenteeism and stoppages were reduced dramatically and productivity increased substantially. It became one of the most productive plants in the Chrysler group.

Ironically, the plant was shut down, not because of its poor industrial relations past, but due to reasons of economies of scale.

From the Linwood experience, the lessons are clear. When groups erect barriers between themselves but still have to live and work together, then one group gains the upper hand over the other. Unfortunately, such a situation lends itself only to short-term thinking and constant crisis management. From management's point of view, it could be more expedient to let the unions have their way in the short term. At least then the dispute would be settled and the plant would quickly be back in próduction. The unintended consequences of such a policy, however, are that management lose control.

From the shopfloor's point of view, the lack of direction from management and management's inability to face crisis meant that the labour force had greater faith in their union representatives. As far as the unions are concerned, they were doing their job. They represented the needs and wishes of their members and struggled to gain improved conditions and pay.

When an organisation is dominated by groups who hold conflicting viewpoints and identify with their own outer-directed values, finding a quick and expedient solution may not always be the answer. Head-on confrontation with the management or union company barons could be the only way out. Seeing a crisis through, giving away as little as possible, may be the only feasible long-term solution.

Keeping the organisation clean

Keeping the organisation clean depends on only handling the 'hygiene factors'. This phrase originates from Professor Herzberg's (1956) two-factor theory. Herzberg pinpointed two factors (stimuli) that influence people's behaviour at work: those factors that dissatisfy and those that satisfy. However, the two factors are not polar opposites. Just because the dissatisfying factors have been handled well does not mean that the satisfying factors are in operation. It is necessary to tackle both. The dissatisfying factors have to be reduced and an alternative strategy has to be practised in order to bring into play the satisfying or motivating factors (Table 4.1).

Hence, concentrating on the hygiene factors makes the place

Table 4.1

Hygiene factors (dissatisfiers)	Motivation factors (satisfiers)
Company policy	Achievement
Administration	Recognition
Supervision	The work itself
Salary	Responsibility
Physical working conditions	Advancement
Interpersonal relations	

clean. Improving the hygiene factors ensures that the basic standard working conditions are tolerable and perhaps even attractive. However, attention to the hygiene factors does not stimulate people to work with greater enthusiasm, drive and energy. To improve performance and output, it is necessary to emphasise the motivation factors: to give people the responsibility and encouragement to do things for themselves.

A strong characteristic of outer-directed organisations is that they only pay attention to the hygiene factors. It is as if they are always trying to get the place cleaner without providing any real stimulus for the future. In certain organisations, motivation factors are even rejected outright. On closer examination, this is no surprise.

What are the rewards? Unless management consciously promote motivation factors, then the only rewards available are the hygiene factors, especially salary and working conditions. With inflation, the introduction of new technologies and the need to respond to fluctuations in the market place, salary and working conditions will always be foremost in people's minds. The problem is that agreements previously reached will always be out of date because of changing circumstances both in the organisation and the market place. In addition, without any debate on the motivation factors, constantly acting on the hygiene factors tends to make the Them and Us barriers seem even bigger.

Group cohesion. After a while, acting on the hygiene factors becomes a dominant norm in the organisation. To offer ideas on alternative ways of handling the situation makes people fearful. Individuals may become anxious because the traditional groupings may be broken down.

The hygiene factors are the forces which enhance group cohesion. If the group sticks together, then pay, company policies and working conditions can be improved. In certain organisations, such a view is held by both management and unions. The traditionalists and company barons have come to dominate both groups.

In contrast, the motivation factors are individualistic and concerned with self-expression. By becoming motivation-oriented, people will need to re-examine their situation and as a result old loyalties, identities and traditions may be swept away.

Understandably, both management and trade unions in some

organisations will reject motivation factors, for if they do not, the status quo could be seriously disrupted. Simply put, the visionaries under such conditions will always be out of favour.

Get your way at whatever cost. In time, people only use two dominant strategies: maintain strict control over your group members; and in conflict with other groups, get your way at whatever cost. The problem with this last strategy is that people can lose sight of what they are trying to achieve.

What to do when the company barons have lost their way

A well-known multinational company, with its headquarters in the UK, has been running at a loss for the last five years. The board members of the company have managed to keep this information secret from their middle managers, the unions and the press. However, the situation had become exceptionally problematic. The company had lost its dominant position in the market, sales were down and forecasted losses were high; the company was just a few steps away from bankruptcy.

In desperation, the chairman of the board invited a marketing consultant to help determine new strategies for the short- to medium-term future. The intervention was successful – new, realistic strategies that would generate substantial income were found. However, the marketing consultant indicated that the company still faced a human resources problem. Management/union relations were very poor. Even though it made eminent sense to pursue the new strategies, there was every likelihood that the unions would not co-operate and even attempt to destroy the new plans. The marketing consultant's recommendation was to bring in a human relations consultant to conduct an industrial relations audit.

The chairman accepted the advice and, after a fairly thorough search, found a consultant that he respected and trusted.

After a few meetings with the human relations consultant, the board agreed to the following strategy:

1 Conduct an organisation-wide human resources audit and not just an industrial relations audit. The consultant considered that there were additional problems at supervisory and middle management levels which required examination.
2 In order to conduct the audit with supervisory and management personnel, four two-day workshops should be organised where a selected number of managers come together at a hotel to discuss and explore the human resources problems facing the company.
3 After each workshop, a report would be written by the consultant and presented to the board.
4 In addition, the consultant would conduct one-to-one/open-ended interviews with a sample of middle managers and supervisors to find out individual views of the company's people problems. Based on the findings of the interviews, a report would be written but without reference to any one individual.

5 Interview a select sample of shop stewards (if access to them could be negotiated) about their views of the company's problems. Again a report would be written for the board summarising the findings and maintaining individual confidentiality.

6 Interview a hand-picked sample of shopfloor operatives to ascertain what they thought was wrong with the company. Again the same conditions concerning confidentiality should be applied.

The consultant conducted himself well. He established a good rapport with the managers he met. The workshops were well organised and valuable information was gathered about the company's present problems and future prospects.

The consultant managed to persuade most shop stewards and some shopfloor operatives to meet him and talk to him. Honest, thought-provoking views were expressed.

A gloomy picture emerged. First, the unions disliked intensely and distrusted immensely, the senior management of the company. Although one or two factories may have co-operated with senior management's plans for expansion, most shop stewards would probably have actively attempted to subvert any attempts at putting the company back on its feet.

The reason for such intense feeling on the union side stemmed from plant closures and redundancies conducted in the mid-1970s. The then more able shop stewards had initiated negotiations with senior management concerning the introduction of new labour-saving equipment and ways of strengthening the company's position in the market place. Quite sincerely, the shop stewards argued for worker/director representation on the main board as a genuine attempt to generate an attitude of partnership between management and shop floor.

Taken aback by the initiative, senior management responded by rejecting the proposals, stating that the real bar to product competitiveness was over-manning. Further, senior management stated they were well able to determine the company's future strategy without union assistance.

Senior management attempted to browbeat the unions into accepting a voluntary redundancy scheme. It was only moderately successful and hence was turned into an enforced redundancy scheme.

Some of the anti-management elements in the unions saw this as an opportunity to vote out some of the existing shop stewards, who had originally offered their initiatives to management. (They were considered Uncle Toms.) In their place were voted individuals with strong anti-management feelings.

Very quickly, strife, strikes, stoppages and low productivity became the norm. Senior management responded by sacking certain members of the union and shop floor and by closing down whole plants. Non-union shopfloor operatives were dismayed. All their efforts that had made the company profitable were now being rewarded by an enforced redundancy scheme. More non-union members joined the union in an attempt to save their jobs.

Some influential middle managers, especially those working at plant level, protested. All their attempts to create profitable factories were now being undermined by rash senior management actions.

The protestors were either moved sideways or sacked. Very quickly, middle management lost faith in senior management. Plant productivity, due to lack of management initiative, fell.

Supervisors and foremen soon lost control of their operatives. Workers and shop stewards quickly recognised that if something needed doing, they should go immediately to higher level management. Supervisors were soon bypassed by the shopfloor and middle management.

Senior management considered their supervisors to be poorly skilled. In order to improve performance, most supervisors were sent on a supervisory skills training programme – to no avail: supervisors had hardly any influence over their teams.

These findings were presented to the board. Most board members reacted angrily. They stated that the opinions expressed were biased and hence the conclusions inaccurate. Two stated openly that the consultant was not much good; a great many more thought it but kept their opinions to themselves. However, the chairman agreed with most of the findings. Despite calls to sack the consultant, he was kept on.

Currently, the chairman and consultant are trying to develop strategies to improve the situation. Some of their tentative ideas are as follows:

1 Sack, or strongly suggest early retirement, for some of the more traditional, obstructive senior managers.

2 Promote the more able middle managers to these vacant positions. Prepare these managers for their new responsibilities by sending them to prestigious business school courses in the UK and USA.

3 Other middle managers and most supervisors should attend a one-week in-company training . programme entitled 'Developing effective working teams' in order to improve their team leadership skills.

4 Strengthen the role of the supervisor by giving them greater authority over quality control, overtime payments and team membership. In addition, middle management should no longer bypass supervisors in their negotiations with the unions.

5 Close down particularly troublesome plants. Management/ shop steward relations in certain factories are considered beyond redemption. Far better to lose the factories and pay out redundancy money than have such disruptive elements in the organisation. If strikes occur as a result, then these have to be fought.

6 Co-operate with the unions to develop a scheme of productivity bonuses if the new marketing strategies prove to be successful.

7 Improve the representative system by supporting worker/ directors on the board.

It remains to be seen whether any of these proposals will be implemented.

None of this would have been necessary had senior management originally considered their status and authority less, the company's position and productivity more and maintained a clear-sighted view of their purpose, instead of losing their way.

Stress: the effect of Them and Us

Stress is the result of negative experiences at work. For the individual, stress refers to personal discomfort and unhappiness. For most stress is a short-term emotional experience. People usually manage to cope with a negative experience. But for some, short-term stress may develop into symptoms of physical anxiety, inability to concentrate, minor physical ailments to longer-term incapacitating diseases. Coronary heart disease is probably the most costly stress-linked disease. Even back in 1973 in the UK, heart ailments accounted for 52 per cent of deaths of men between 45–54 years and 41 per cent of men between 24–44 years of age. Stress is a major worry to people in both public and private sector organisations, for as Cooper (1983) has indicated, stress-related illnesses are increasing.

Researchers have found that the individual's work environment plays an important role in stimulating stressful experiences. Several studies have concluded (see selective bibliography for Chapter 4) that stress is low in organisations of under 50 persons but can reach quite intolerable levels in large organisations (i.e. more than 1,000 persons). The problem seems to be that people are hampered by too many bosses, too many controls, too much paperwork, i.e. too much bureaucracy. Unfortunately, stress cannot be eradicated simply by reducing the size of organisations. Not only would the economic consequences of such a move be disastrous, but further, public service organisations which have generated high expectations, may then not be able to meet their basic commitments.

The alternative would seem to be to give departments/divisions/sub-units in the organisation more autonomy. However, as indicated in the discussion on size of organisations in Chapter 3 (see section on Small *v* large: was size ever a choice?), decentralisation would give rise to a need for greater co-ordination which, unless skilfully handled, could become impossible as groups, departments and divisions are often out of the control and co-ordinative power of those at the top.

Stress will not be alleviated simply by centralising or decentralising. Role conflict, role ambiguity, poor relationships with superiors and subordinates and lack of career development are the important stress factors the larger an organisation becomes.

Committing professional suicide by Dr Don Cole (1981)

Don Cole, social worker, psychologist, consultant and entrepreneur, recently wrote a fascinating book, entitled *Professional Suicide*. He states that professional self-destruction takes place in most organisations. Don calls it organisational murder. It happens when the brightest and most committed employees get killed off, in a professional sense, by the organisation that most needs their talents. The symptoms of professional suicide are when people:

- leave and take another job below their level of qualifications and experience;
- cause an uproar which is likely to destroy their career or even get them the sack;
- look forward to early retirement;
- fail to grow with the job and become obsolete when new technology leaves them behind;
- let themselves physically degenerate, by becoming fat, sleepy or nervous.

Cole draws heavily on his own experiences as a professional psychologist, hired by a Cleveland aerospace firm (USA) to find out why young go-getters were either leaving in large numbers or becoming ineffective on the job.

Cole concluded that the predominant management style in the company was paternalistic. What employees need is supervision by mature people so that most can get to grips with their job and generally be given encouragement, direction and support. Paternalistic management cannot provide such a sophisticated atmosphere within the organisation.

Cole does not just criticise. He provides a way out. His recommendation is to introduce 'circular management'. This involves making teams out of committees, openly confronting sensitive issues and problems, developing more colleague relations than boss–worker relations and sharing authority and responsibility.

Cole is implying that greater notice should be taken of the team coach. How is that possible with outer-directed people; the company baron especially? One commonly pursued strategy for improving the situation in many organisations has been to place greater emphasis on human resource training and development.

The human resource specialist: combating Them and Us

Substantial interest and investment have been given to the development of people at work. It has been recognised that with ever-increasing size and the ever-increasing specialisation and

professionalisation of tasks, effective performance at work could
no longer be left to the total discretion of the individual or to
good fortune.

The more successful companies in the USA took a close look
at their people-processing departments and began to split
separate functions into separate units. Training and development became a separate entity from company administration,
wages administration and keeping records.

By contrast, in most organisations in the UK, the people
processing functions fall under the same umbrella, the personnel
department. The difference is that in the USA, the development
of the human resource is a business decision to obtain business
ends. In the UK, the situation is not so clear-cut.

Changes in social policy

Changes made in social policy in the 1960s and 1970s in the UK
clearly influenced the role of personnel management. From the
late 1950s to the mid 1970s, politicians, administrators and
academics fought to improve the lot of their fellow citizens.
What were seen as welfare privileges were turned into rights
backed by legislation. The personnel officer found that some of
his activities were prescribed by law. The personnel officer
became the custodian of the employer's legal duties to his
employees. In addition, again due to legislation, the personnel
officer had to get himself involved in employee participation
schemes. He found himself in a somewhat nebulous role
between trying to develop a close relationship with management
and with the unions and trying to lead them into areas which
one or both may have been reluctant to enter.

Such a background has produced two interesting results in
the UK.

First result: personnel management's emphasis on crisis
management. The conditions under which a person is employed
and what he can and cannot do are generally controlled by
statute or by agreement between two or more parties – a form of
social contract.

Negotiating social contracts has been the centre of controversy
for the last 30 years. Acceptable conditions at work have come
through collective bargaining and negotiation between
management, trade unions, staff associations etc. The problem
is that an agreement does not last for long enough. In the larger

UK organisations, agreements on pay and working conditions are usually upheld for a year. More often than not, as soon as agreements are reached, the round of negotiations starts again for the next year. In addition, agreements are not universally made. Agreements reached between management and one union may not be the same as between management and another union. The reasons for discrepancies in pay agreements often make sense. People with differing skills, levels of responsibility or differences in working conditions should be rewarded differently. However, as soon as one group sees itself being treated differently from another, problems arise. People do not wish to stick to their agreements but attempt to re-negotiate their position, upset the status quo which triggers off a whole cycle of negotiations.

Under such circumstances, personnel managers become industrial relations negotiators. In effect, they become expert at handling crisis management, but forget about longer-term strategy.

Yesterday's company baron tomorrow

The personnel director of a multinational food processing and manufacturing company decided that the company's image needed updating. His directive to his staff – determine the type of executive we will need tomorrow and recruit him today. The task was not easy. The company was massive. It is, in reality, a loose confederation of different companies, each with quite different identities and traditions. Further, the senior managers in personnel all came from an industrial relations background. They all prided themselves on being expert managers who could handle crises. The central personnel department was considered an efficient administrative unit but not too enlightened in terms of generating new ideas.

One of the senior managers suggested that psychometric/personality tests should be used to identify, first, what sort of managers the company had in its employ and second, what sort of managers should it hire in the future? The company opted to use one test only. An outside consultant was hired to advise on the use of the test.

His first advice – forget the test altogether. If you really want to find the executive of the future, a far more in-depth study of the organisation would be required. One test can in no way assess what is really happening in the organisation or what you want.

The personnel director did not listen. He wanted a quick result. The personnel team went ahead with the project. Without proper preparation or warning, both line managers and graduate recruits were asked to complete the test. Although it was clearly stated that all results would be kept in the strictest confidence, many refused to complete the test. Once line management became more aware of the project, they openly opposed it. 'How could one test measure what was really happening in the organisation and why were they not consulted in the planning of the project?', they demanded to know.

The net result was that the project was disbanded. Line management lost faith in the personnel department and appointed staff without consulting personnel. Line managers appointed the type of staff they knew and understood – practical, hard-working, get the job done, no-nonsense people.

The net result is that yesterday's company barons are being appointed for tomorrow.

Even today, the personnel director does not accept that it was his inability at handling longer-term strategies that was at fault.

Second result: personnel management's emphasis on systems management. With the pressure of constant crisis management, the need for rationality and order has become a priority. Personnel managers have ended up managing organisation structures and systems, at times to the exclusion of all else. The bulk of personnel work has concentrated on:

- dividing tasks into specific jobs or specialised offices which could then be defined with some precision:
- relying on the hierarchy to make co-ordination of diverse tasks possible:
- establishing the role holder's position with defined rules and procedures:
- attempting to assess people on dubious job performance criteria:
- developing a structured pattern of hierarchical promotion and calling it career development.

Such established rationality and order has become more important than new challenges. Instead of the system being administered to help the people in their job, pressure is applied to ensure regularity of behaviour even when evidence exists that change is required.

How do you learn?

Professors Argyris and Schon (1978) of Harvard and MIT respectively, offer the hypothesis that probably everyone learns from the past and from their mistakes. However, it is the depth of learning that really counts.

Certain individuals and organisations learn only by trying to detect errors, then correct them and continue to strive for current objectives. Such learning is termed *single-loop* learning. Single-loop learning tends to be shallow and only of limited use. When a single mistake has been made, single-loop learning can be applied to correct the error.

However, when policies and strategies are being re-examined, single-loop learning is inappropriate. *Double-loop* learning is required. Double-loop learning involves examining the underlying norms, policies and objectives of the organisation. It may involve coming up with something entirely new.

Argyris and Schon are sceptical whether the conditions in today's organisations are conducive to double-loop learning. Even the people development specialists in organisations are not aware of the value of double-loop learning.

The power of the company baron

For the company baron, the situation is ideal. Why? First, Outer-directed values predominate in organisations. One reason is size. Another is the inability of people to appreciate the complexities of today's organisations.

Further, people only seem to work on the symptoms and not the underlying causes. In Argyris and Schon's terms, many of today's organisations seem only to practise *single-loop* learning: developing expertise in error detection and error correction even though a fundamental re-examination of basic issues is required.

Neither have the human resource specialists been able to alter the situation. After all, they, like anyone else, have to live and survive in today's organisations. To enter into double-loop learning is not only impractical but could be seen as revolutionary. Through no particular fault of their own, the personnel people contribute as much as anyone to the 'them and us' barrier.

The company baron is at his most powerful. For that reason, we must stop and re-examine our organisations.

5 Re-examining Organisations

Far too many people at work are faced with a loss of purpose. When they feel they are no longer in control of what they do or how they do it (loss of self-direction); when they feel pushed into behaving in ways their peers and superiors find acceptable (pressure for consistency), then they have lost their own and the organisation's sense of purpose. It becomes virtually impossible to answer the question, 'why is the organisation doing the things it is, in the way it does?'

Size of organisation and a preoccupation with organisation structures have been found to be the two most important reasons. As already explained in the last two chapters, with increases in size arises the need to structure activities so as to achieve some semblance of order and co-ordination. The greater the number of roles, procedures and rules, the greater the complexity in organisations. Soon, professional, financial and role structures become intertwined, leaving people in a state of confusion as to what is being done, and where.

As a result, measurement rather than purpose become the order of the day. Whether it be output or job-related performance, as long as it can be measured according to predetermined criteria, then the individual or the unit or group must be making a worthwhile contribution.

In an attempt to justify existing structures through quantification, there has been a loss of qualitative feeling and intuition. People's abilities to use their own insights and examine why things are being done the way they are, are diminished in the face of 'hard' data which appear to justify the status quo.

In effect, what has been achieved are dependency-inducing relationships as opposed to creative, free-thinking ideas.

Too great a reliance has been placed on the organisation to satisfy fundamental status and motivational needs. There is pressure on people to adopt the values of the traditionalist and company baron. As a result of abdicating responsibility to the organisation, we have ceased to think about the longer-term future and the opportunities and problems it will bring.

Both our organisational structures and the attitudes we have developed to suit those structures are outdated. Today, we are no longer living in an economy where one can accurately predict the size of the market and the product life cycle of the goods and services we sell. We can no longer afford to live with our old attitudes and organisation structures. We are faced with rapid technological change, competition and ever-increasing national political involvement in business decisions.

To respond to the challenge of political and economic change, we must try to predict the organisational structures and shapes of the future and explore the impact that certain innovations are having on our way of life.

INNOVATION, DECLINE AND NEW GROWTH

Innovation

André Piatier (1981) states that the western world has extended into the third industrial revolution due to the innovations that have already taken place: new energy sources, new means of transport and new means of communication. Most of us are aware of the increasing pace of technological change yet few of us are aware of its enormity. Skimping through some of the literature of futurism makes interesting reading. Did you know that:

- in the USA 6,000 new food products are generated each year;
- 90 per cent of all consumer goods in 1975 were totally unknown in 1900;
- it is estimated that 70 per cent of the consumer goods to be sold in 1986 have not yet been invented;
- 80 per cent of the products and 90 per cent of the profits made in the German machine-tool industry have come from new ideas generated in the last decade and not from immediate post-world war II practices;

- knowledge doubled between 1800 and 1900; it doubled again between 1950 and 1960; it doubled again between 1960 and 1966; since then it has been impossible to keep track of its growth;
- 90 per cent of all scientists that ever lived are alive today (estimated 5 million);
- in 2000 AD it is estimated that there will be at least 25 million scientists;
- in California, a group of scientists is developing ways of utilising solar energy to the extent of providing all the power and energy the USA needs. Coal, oil and gas are likely to become redundant. The scientists estimate that by using the hydrogen in solar energy to generate controlled nuclear explosions, this in turn will produce sufficient power for domestic and industrial requirements. Energy on such an enormous scale could become a viable proposition within the next five years;
- developments in micro-electronics, robotics and tele-communications will have far reaching effects over the next 15 years. The information revolution has already introduced new, cheap and easy-to-use methods of data storage, retrieval and analysis. Automation is now in our offices with word processors, desktop VDU's (visual display units) and facsimile transmission.

The end result will be that head office will become more impotent whilst branch offices will increase in importance.

Only just round the corner are the telephone-linked view data systems whereby the individual at home will be linked not only with other individuals both by sight and sound but also with information systems; such systems will eventually replace many reference books and journals.

Robotics has changed the world of manufacturing. Automation (a combination of robotics and micro-electronics) has made a major impact in production processes, warehousing and stock control.

Changing face of the factory

In the automotive industry, the exception today is the car plant that does not use robots. Fiat not only use robots for car production but have masterminded a marketing campaign for the sale of the Fiat Strada around the theme of 'hand-built by robots'.

Ford UK have installed 30 robots at the Halewood plant for their new Escort line, whilst British Leyland have gone a long way to automating their Mini-Metro line at Longbridge. In the USA, General Motors are ordering robots by the hundreds.

Although robots have been in operation since the 1960s it is only recently that they have become an important consideration in the production process. In the car industry, robots are currently being used for spot welding, pressure diecasting, plastic injection moulding, paint and powder spraying, forging, loading and unloading metal cutting machines, press loading and unloading, investment costing and heat treatment.

At present, the robot cannot see, hear or speak. However, the crude robots we have are taking over the human work load to the extent of 3 robots to 60 human beings.

The more intelligent robot of the future is already in operation in Japan. The Yamazaki machine-tool factory near Nagoya claims that it has devised a system whereby the entire operations of the factory, including accounting, the preparation of financial statements and production control, can be managed automatically. The system, already in use for the manufacture of certain machine tools, is worked in three shifts: the first shift employs seven people, the second shift requires five people and the night shift runs without anybody. A report in the *Financial Times* (19 May 1981) estimated that present world sales in robots is around $350m but the market should be worth $2bn and upwards by 1990.

Decline

Innovation may be exciting but it also brings decline. That decline is with us.

Certain futurologists estimate that with the advent of micro-electronics, 3–5 million people will be made redundant as automated machine systems substitute human labour. Current political opinion in both the US and the UK is that if both countries adopt micro-electronics more slowly than their competitors, then the effects would be more painful than 3–5 million unemployed.

The futurologist Keith Pavitt (1980) urges more rapid change for Britain. If the UK does not adopt sophisticated automated production systems as in Japan, then it will have to rely, in part, on human labour. Third world countries in South East Asia and Latin America will soon capture our markets as their use of cheap labour and the application of intermediate technologies in areas ranging from textiles, shoes and clothing to bulk chemical, steel and consumer durable products will mean cheaper goods for sale. Pavitt's message is clear, either change or miss even more opportunities.

The situation has been made more difficult over the last

decade. Changes in political and economic conditions have substantially shortened the forward planning time horizons of many organisations. Commodity prices and supplies have fluctuated continually and widely in response to political developments. There have been substantial fluctuations of price and supplies in sugar, coffee and cocoa, leaving the confectionery industry, for example, in an uncertain state.

Market swings in copper prices have created problems for management in the non-ferrous metal industries. Inflated prices for raw materials leads to uncertainties about consumer behaviour. Will people buy at a higher price? Will wholesalers and retailers purchase bulk orders in anticipation of price rises and horde and release spasmodically in order to make greater profits? Will the customer find a substitute product and thereby lessen the real demand for the original product?

Perhaps the most dramatic fluctuations have been in the world's oil industry. Oil prices remained stable until the Arab/Israeli war of 1974. By 1982, there were substantial fluctuations in price with the average OPEC price being $34.25 per barrel, Saudi Arabia charging $34.36 and Algeria, Libya and Nigeria shifting between that and $41.00 per barrel. In 1983, the price of oil plummeted.

For the businessman, the topsy-turvy world oil has certainly made a direct impact on his trading. For Sir Derek Ezra, former Chairman of the British National Coal Board, the future is somewhat promising. Speaking at the energy conference in Montreux, Switzerland (May 1981) he said, 'UK coal would be providing petrol for motorists, jet fuel for aircraft and feedstocks for chemical plants'.

In contrast, many small garage owners have gone out of business during the last six years. Those more entrepreneurial recognised that cars run as well on butane gas as on petrol. A good source of revenue have been gas conversions, whereby motor vehicles can be propelled by both gas and petrol.

The gas conversion business has probably been best applied by the small garage owner in the Republic of Ireland where petrol is (approx) £1.00 dearer than in the UK and three times the price in the USA.

The chemicals industry has also suffered, for it is oil rather than coal or natural gas that is the important energy source. At present, the chemicals industry has to base its future development on uncertain capital costs and even more uncertain raw materials and energy costs.

The net result is that decline and development go hand in hand. The process of discarding unwanted systems and skills has to be combined with developing innovative ideas for the future. To improve our lot, we must be able to handle two processes simultaneously: the management of decline and the management of new growth.

Management of decline

The management of decline involves cutting back, closing down, lowering overhead costs, reducing the size of work forces through redundancy, retirement schemes and job placement services. The process involves breaking down old structures and coping with anxieties, those of others and one's own.

Politics of making sweets

An old-fashioned sweet-manufacturing company in the North of England is facing problems. The company has been producing a particular type of sweet for the last 60 years. The company built its reputation on this product range as a high-quality, mass-output, low-cost sweet, a favourite in the UK and Europe. The sweet is still a favourite but sales are falling quite dramatically.

The problem is cost. The sweet is now marginally too expensive for its market. Traditionally the sweet was sold neatly packaged at the corner tobacconist/newsagent shop to mothers and children. With the growth of the supermarket and with increasing overhead costs the company increased its prices in excess of other high-quality, low-cost sweets. Orders fell dramatically.

The problem of costs is related to the inefficient modes of production currently in use. Machinery still well capable of doing the job is, however, old and has been in use for the last 40 to 50 years. It has now become inefficient. Great reliance is placed on human labour but the problem here is overmanning. The company employs two to three times the number of people it requires for the same quantity of production with the same machinery. It is a traditional company, firmly believing in protecting its labour force from redundancy.

The director of personnel, recognising the problem, hired an aggressive factory manager (visionary) to put right one of the least profitable factories located 120 miles from head office. The factory manager stated that the factory units, its old machinery and overmanned and aged work force would never be profitable. He set about closing down the factory, negotiating redundancy agreements, selling machinery and ensuring that no strike occurred in the factory which could spread to the rest of the group. He successfully achieved all four objectives within nine months.

The director of personnel then transferred him to another factory not more than 35 miles from head office, with the same brief. In this case, the factory manager considered that the factory could

become profitable if a programme of rationalisation was implemented. Large-scale redundancies were enforced, old machinery
was sold, new machinery brought in and a small but highly skilled
labour force was hired. The labour force at the second factory
offered more resistance. A strike was organised which lasted for five
weeks. The factory manager spent considerable time negotiating
with the Chief Executive and colleagues to ensure that he had their
support. Eventually the strike broke down. Now, two years later, the
factory is one of the most profitable in the group serving home and
foreign markets.

Currently, the director of personnel is trying to transfer the
factory manager to head office which is located on the same site as
the oldest, largest and probably most unprofitable factory in the
group. The chief executive feels uneasy about the transfer.

The chief executive is the archetypal company baron. Other
directors and managers have openly opposed the transfer, stating
that the factory manager is nothing more than a hatchet man.

The chief executive has successfully opened two factories in the
USA and is considering starting a new, but small, factory in North
Scotland. In an attempt to escape the problems at home, the chief
executive is at present negotiating with the factory manager to
transfer him to factory manager (North Scotland factory).

The chief executive is reported to have said, 'For Christ's sake,
get this guy out of my hair. He worries me every time I see him!'

If your boss is a company baron, the last thing you do is too much,
too quickly and too well!

From the above case, the key features of the management of
decline can be outlined:

1 *Break down old identities.* Well-established units, factories,
divisions and even whole companies are likely to have developed
a particular identity, supportive of its own people but suspicious
of all new influences from outside that could be disruptive to the
group. Both management and work force make no allowances
for changes in work patterns and work practice to cope with
external market conditions. Traditionalist values come to the
fore.

Under such circumstances, it is no use blaming the shop floor
for adopting restrictive work practices. Management are just as
guilty. To combat such a situation, old structures must be
broken down, with the unfortunate but inevitable consequences of redundancies and early retirements. The traditionalists and their patrons – the company barons – must go!

Effective cutting back has to apply to both management and
the shop floor.

2 *Confront the conflict.* In managing the decline of any

organisation, conflicts will arise. When evolutionary measures no longer apply, the inevitable conflict must be confronted.

Traditional groupings of people need to be broken down, work practices changed, many made redundant, for some with little prospect of gaining new employment, for others enforced transfer to another part of the organisation.

Whilst confronting the conflict, the change agent(s) must gather support for his cause. Traditionally, organisational conflict has been seen in terms of management v the work force. That is simply inaccurate. As much dislike and mistrust exists and has existed between senior and middle managers as between management and work force. The ideal of corporate identity, although palatable in times of growth, is exposed as a myth in times of decline. Hence, any manager embarking on a policy of conflict and confrontation should spend as much, if not more, of his time negotiating support from his peers and superiors as well as attempting to negotiate a settlement with the other conflicting parties. The senior management of any organisation will harbour doubts and anxieties about actively supporting a policy of direct confrontation, even if there is no feasible, positive alternative. The situation could so easily get out of their control.

As the factory manager in the case above discovered, support may be offered but not necessarily given when required. He had continually to negotiate and re-negotiate his position with his bosses. He partially succeeded; others have not! When the situation becomes too uncomfortable, your own peers may remove you.

3 *Establish the new system.* By rationalising out the old, surviving the inevitable conflict, it is then necessary to establish the new system.

The new system is composed of the new strategies, new organisation structures, new specialists and operatives hired to stimulate growth and development. To generate the drive and motivation to do new things, then the new system really must be new. It is not worth sacking some of the old work force and a certain number of supervisors and middle managers but retaining the upper echelons of the hierarchy. The reason why the previous situation deteriorated was that senior management were not in control or were unaware of both internal and external conditions. Reorganisation without a fundamental change of management is a wasted exercise, and there will be no trust between the various levels in the organisation.

For a manager embarking on a policy of rapid re-organisation and development, it is worth considering whether he has a hard core of supporters ready to form the new order. The factory manager in the case above did not, when it came to head office support. Although fundamentally successful, the factory manager made the senior directors in the company anxious. Their inability either to manage conflicts strategically or to confront them was exposed. Without a well-established support group, the factory manager is likely to be sent to North Scotland as a reward for his endeavours.

Management of new growth

In contrast to the management of reduction, the management of new growth is concerned with innovation, experimentation, free-wheeling ideas, flexibility of response rather than a standardisation of systems. The management of new growth involves three areas of consideration:

- the organisation structures of the future;
- flexibility of purpose;
- importance of work.

Structuring future organisations. Three separate organisation structures are likely to emerge or are already in operation: integral structure, federal structure and satellite project structure.

Integral structure is already in operation. Its feature is that it depends on planning and decision making being conducted at the centre. Supply, manufacturing and distribution arrangements are controlled from the centre. Subsidiaries, outlying units and factories are treated as operational units being provided with central services to conduct their business.

The difference between an integral structured organisation and a centralised organisation is the flexibility of response to changing market conditions. Central office would require an efficient management information system so as to enable managers to set realistic targets for their locality. To prevent frustration and to keep in touch with the centre, local managers would have to be transferred to the centre and to the various subsidiaries at reasonably regular intervals on mutually acceptable contracts. It is unrealistic and demoralising to move people around with little chance of promotion, higher income,

status or extra-monetary rewards. Self-negotiated contracts
would provide the individual manager with the choice of what
rewards he would wish to pursue.

An integral structured organisation can only operate
effectively when considerable investment is given to generating
effective management development systems. Whether on-or
off-the-job training programmes are organised, the objective is
still the same – to help people identify with the organisation and
to make the necessary movement of personnel challenging and
not just acceptable.

Federal structure, the complete opposite to the integral
structured organisation, is a loose mixture of companies, units
or divisions, linked by a common factor, whereby each unit of
the federation will be independent of the centre. Co-operation
rather than control will be the dominant management style.
The only limit to the autonomy of each unit would be a central
servicing function providing a range of facilities such as
management information and market research data; a central
personnel, recruitment and training service to be utilised when
required; a management services/internal consultancy service
available to all members of the federation for on-the-job
problem solving; a central planning unit advising and directing
new capital investment through a co-ordinated planning system
throughout the federation.

Such a system is already (if somewhat unsuccessfully) in
operation. Some multinationals have developed a system where
local units can develop their own policies and make their own
decisions to suit local conditions. Other companies have found
they have no alternative but to adopt a collaborative rather than a
centralised structure. The food giant, Cadbury's Schweppes,
which produces and markets products from fizzy drinks to teas
to jams and jellies, has a federal structure in operation.
Managers identify with their particular division and if need be
will act independently of head office. Other multinationals
which have diversified into fields outside their traditional
product range have found it of greater advantage not to interfere
too much with their new acquisitions. Often the original
company name with its existing management are maintained.
Greater emphasis is placed on integrating the company into the
federation.

The only real option for managing the large organisation of
the future is likely to be the federal system. Advances in

communication and information transmission, sensitivity to local conditions and the need to respond to competition and market swings make collaboration and negotiation the best styles to adopt. The need for flexibility is likely to be maintained.

However, the key to operating a federally structured organisation successfully is to ensure that each of the federal units has sufficient loyalty to the centre so that some sort of cohesion is maintained throughout the group. Loyalty to the centre can be achieved by introducing a feeling of competition between the units, but with the centre being firmly in control of the outcome. In additon, well thought through management development systems and programmes will help towards promoting entrepreneurially minded managers who can agree with central policies.

Most of the multinationals that operate a federal structure have still not succeeded in creating an effective management development system that will stimulate line managers to have a positive identity with the centre. Developing well thought through human resources strategies for large organisations is a major challenge.

Satellite project structure. With innovations in products and services; with more intense competition facing business organisations, the need for experimental, *ad hoc* units devised for specific purposes, will grow. Teams of professionals will be assembled to work on particular projects. The teams need to be given sufficient independence to make both tactical and strategic decisions in so far as they affect the project.

The success of projects will depend on the project manager's ability to remain independent of the parent organisation. The problem-solving culture of the project team will only be enhanced if task-oriented professionals debate the problems and objectives they face without having to consider lines of accountability and authority, confusion over task responsibilities or the possibility of blame by senior management when things begin to go wrong.

The principles on which such teams would operate are:

- encourage persons of different professional backgrounds to become team members;
- ensure that the team adopts a true task-oriented culture and is free from bureaucratic influence by making decisions and acting independently of the parent organisation;

- the model of operation of the satellite team has to be problem-oriented as opposed to working on routine matters. The aim of the team is to operate as a multi-disciplinary unit in an interdisciplinary style and co-operate with relevant outside agencies;
- there should only be one accountability line within the team. The person at the head of the team is accountable for the practices and activities of all personnel within the unit;
- the team or unit should be relatively small with possibly one or more teams within the same geographical area;
- offices in which the teams are located should be set apart from the parent organisation;
- members of the team should work full-time within the teams, possibly seconded from the parent organisation for periods of one to three years, or even be employed as permanent members of the team;
- generate a career hierarchy within the teams which individual professional members could strive to climb, based on competent work with clients. The hierarchy should be shallow, and whether at the top or bottom of the hierarchy all members of the team should be practitioners and not just administrators.

Above all, for satellite project structures to operate effectively they must be given the freedom to operate independently of head office.

Flexibility of purpose. With rapid developments in information technology and systems and the more demanding competitive style likely to be adopted in the future, organisations will have to be more flexible about their purpose. Some are; others have refused to be.

'We are engineers, not property developers' said the company baron

A multinational telecommunications company had contracted with a business school to provide for all their advanced management training.

At one of the management programmes, when some of the company's managers were discussing the problems of handling foreign subsidiaries, one of the managers stated that the biggest problem at one of their South East Asian locations was suitable accommodation for their managers and engineers.

Most of the company's staff are married and have children. Their placements abroad could last for up to 20 years. Naturally wives and families follow the husband out to his foreign location. At this particular South East Asian port of call, suitable accommodation had been found for the managers, engineers and their families, but the company was paying exceptionally high rents.

The manager who posed tne problem added that the company had made a mistake some years back by selling houses and blocks of luxury flats that it owned in this locality. At the time, the reason given was that upkeep would have been too much of a burden and too costly. Now these properties would have been a tremendous saving for the company. One of the company's directors sitting at the back of the lecture room stated:

'My dear fellow, you must realise we are engineers not property developers!'

Someone else in the room replied that profits in that locality could be higher by 35 per cent had the company's directorate adopted a more flexible purpose.

Incidentally, the company director above has completed the politics self-inventory questionnaire (Chapter 1) and to his surprise, but not mine, he scored exceptionally high as a company baron.

Developing greater flexibility of purpose must involve considering the following areas: the means of control; the drive for new responsibility; the need to innovate.

Means of control. How will managers manage? More than likely through processes of collaboration and co-operation, with less emphasis on control. Sophistication in automation and systems of production not unnaturally induces sophistication in the manner of conducting relationships at work. Bob Ramsay, former industrial relations director of Ford (UK) advocated in a recent article in the *Financial Times* that industrial harmony, the key to company profitability, could be achieved only through mutual respect and trust.

Ramsay must have been observing developments in the USA where the Ford United Autoworkers Union (UAW) and Ford management have negotiated a deal which involves profit sharing based on productivity and a guarantee to workers with 15 years' service to the company, significant earnings even if the worker is laid off. Today, 17 million US workers participate in some form of profit-sharing plan.

Management will no longer simply be able to apply control in the future. Control will only be pertinent when coupled with collaboration and both will only be acceptable when senior management can justify their decisions and actions to the other management, supervisory and work force grades. It is not just adopting a new style, but more a maturing of attitude.

New responsibility. From the early 1970s onwards, more companies recognised that they could no longer depend on their original field of expertise for profit generation. The more alert companies diversified into new fields.

In the UK, traditional brewery companies are slowly, but surely, buying into the business of foreign travel and leisure.

American oil companies have diversified into areas ranging from coal mining to farming.

British American Tobacco (BAT) has been diversifying into the US retailing trade. In the summer of 1982 it bought Marshal Field, the Chicago-based department store chain, for £172m. Strangest of all is the recent (1982) and successful bid (worth $160m) by American Brands, a diversified tobacco company, for Pinkerton's, the biggest and the best in the detective agency business.* Buying the brand name seems to be just as important as the product.

Diversification can be effective, but is certainly not new. Management buy-outs, however, are. Management buy-outs involve some employees of a company, often the executives, joining with financial institutions to buy the business or part of it from its present owners. So far, the financial institutions have been content to offer most of the finance in the form of debt and preferred capital but take only a small part of the equity. The managers put all their capital into the business and are allowed to run the business in their own way.

Clearing banks and merchant banks seem to favour these schemes. Barclays Bank has invested some £6m in 13 buy-outs between 1979 and 1982.

For the managers themselves, once they have come to terms with the risk they take, they seem to prefer buy-outs to running subsidiaries. For them, head office charges too much for its services. They prefer to be given a free hand and take a calculated risk.

Management buy-outs are all part of the process of deconglomeration, where ownership of the business and not just control provides the fundamental drive to action.

Need for innovation. Chris Lorenz (1982) wrote a captivating article indicating that innovation and design are Britain's missing link. Britain is falling far behind European, Japanese and US competitors in the design of new products.

For Mrs Thatcher, the problem is of sufficient concern for her to have held a seminar with senior executives from British

---

* Source: *Financial Times,* 8 December 1982.

industry to examine why industrial decision makers seem to fail to appreciate the long-term vital contribution that new designs can make to a company's success.

Lorenz points out that from a wide range of consumer products, Britain offered only three that seemed attractive to home and foreign markets: the Land Rover, BL's Mini-Metro and Clarks Polyvildt shoes. Other products ranging from shavers, coffee makers, typewriters and televisions are foreign-built, but popular in the British market. Why should Britain be lacking in product innovation? In 1983, he answered the question; designers are not given sufficient influence in management.

Perhaps the company barons at lunch can show us why.

The company barons at lunch

The director of personnel and the training manager of an international paint corporation were discussing their new management development strategy for the group with an outside consultant. They were considering hiring him to assist them refine their new management development strategy. The three were at lunch. The consultant seemed satisfied that all features of management development were adequately covered except one!

'What of innovation and design for the future?' asked the consultant.

'Too expensive. Would have to spend too much on R and D! Anyhow, the chief executive would want results fairly quickly and what's the point; our German subsidiary has always done better in this area. They think it, and we produce it!' replied the director of personnel.

'Do you completely own the German subsidiary?' asked the consultant.

'No, only 51 per cent. Don't worry, they have been with us for some time', replied the director of personnel.

'I suppose one or two Germans sit on the main board to influence policy', commented the consultant.

'Not at all, my good chap. You see, we have tried that but they don't seem to fit. Anyhow I know what you are thinking, things will be allright! We get on just fine', stated the director of personnel.

The consultant did not say it, but he thought it – for how long?

Importance of work. I recently conducted three seminars, all entitled, 'The importance of work', with three separate groups; senior managers, supervisors and shopfloor operatives, and a group of unemployed managers and shopfloor operatives. All members were asked to name the two most important developmental experiences they could remember and log down how they felt at the time. Their experiences are interesting (see Table 5.1).

Table 5.1

Senior Managers		Supervisors/Operatives		Unemployed	
Experience	Feelings	Experience	Feelings	Experience	Feelings
Promotion	Exhilaration	Being offered a job	Relief, gain self-respect	Redundancy	Hate, fear, suicidal, depression, let down, what to do with my time?
Winning a contract	Challenging, joy	Doing a good job	Self satisfaction		
Demotion	Depression	Being in work	Secure, making a contribution	Searching for jobs	Depressing, hopeful, being knocked down, loss of self-respect, mistrust the system which allows high unemployment
Praise for a good job done	Superb, handle anything				

112

Over 90 per cent of the experiences offered concerned work. The feelings expressed by all three groups were deep and meaningful.

Nothing seemed to create more exhilaration than some form of advancement at work. Equally, nothing seemed more depressing than demotion or redundancy. Those people that spend a fair proportion of their income on social pastimes are in employment. Those not gainfully employed spend their increased leisure hours trying to find suitable employment. Enjoyable leisure occurs when people are satisfied with their work.

Even those people who worked on repetitive, meaningless tasks and were then made redundant, stated that eventually they too demanded work but more meaningful work. After a while, they did not know what to do with their time whilst unemployed.

Recent developments in the UK mining industry have shown what miners will do to keep their jobs.

Rejecting the mining union's company baron

At the 1982 annual organisation development network (ODN) conference (UK), one of the speakers, an unpaid National Union of Mineworkers official, talked about recent developments in the relationship between the union and its members.

The recently elected president of the union – Arthur Scargill – had argued that the Coal Board should be persuaded to accept an over 20 per cent pay claim for all mining worker grades. At the time, this was a high pay claim. Most pay settlements in other industries ranged from 5 – 8 per cent.

Certain senior mining union officials did not wish to pursue such a policy, for it could only result in a bitter strike with the employers. The end result could well be that many miners would be made redundant. It was decided that a secret ballot be held amongst all the members. The result: 60 per cent against the pay claim; 40 per cent for the claim. An unusual occurrence: the membership voting against its president.

According to the NUM official speaking at the conference, the miners were worried about losing their jobs. It was felt that under the present economic conditions, the Coal Board could not, or would not, endorse such a high pay claim and would also use the pay issue as an excuse to make miners redundant and close down unprofitable pits.

Working down the mines is not the most attractive of occupations. Yet miners preferred to keep their jobs, go against their union president and negotiate for only small increases rather than face unemployment, the dole, means tests for state benefits and a loss of self-respect.

Being in work is so very important.

It has taken us a long time to understand that work is probably one of the most developmental and growth-enhancing experiences of our lives. Even with the advent of new labour-saving technologies, the importance of work will not be diminished. People will demand work which fulfils their needs. People want to feel they are making a contribution. People will not be satisfied with just a series of mundane tasks.

Certain organisations are well aware of the importance of work. When the multinational, ICI, was faced with the prospect of making staff redundant in the early 1970s, they attempted to find alternative jobs for their departing staff. One of their personnel staff recently stated that the trickle had become a deluge and they could no longer cope. Redundancy for ICI has now taken on a more negative connotation. No alternative jobs are now being found.

Other companies such as Whitbread, the UK brewer, have hired a redundancy consultant to provide counselling, advice on redundancy payments and, most of all, a job placement service for its surplus work force. The company seems to have accepted its social responsibility and gone about easing the pain of redundancy in an energetic way.

Organisations will be forced to accept greater social responsibility for the provision of adequate employment.

Work is an exceptionally powerful determinant of personal satisfaction.

Acting on the key issues

To summarise, the organisations of the future will have to handle decline and growth simultaneously. Decline and growth involve:

Decline	*Growth*
– redundancies	– greater flexibility
– departures	– smaller organisational units
– breaking trust	– intuition and innovation
– breaking down old identities	– less control, more collaboration
	– less dependence on organisation
– establishing new order	– more dependence on self
	– need for satisfying work

Outer-directed values are being broken down. What will replace them? Perhaps other outerdirected values. However, the point is that the way we think and do things now needs to change so that we can prepare ourselves for the future.

The block is the company baron, for he is the skilled champion of the status quo. It is ironic that at one time, the company baron was in demand. His manoeuvres, deals and energy kept the organisation on course; the organisation remained a useful, productive, profitable entity. In Argyris and Schon's terms (Chapter 4), the company baron has propounded single-loop learning. However, certain dramatic changes have taken place. Organisations need now to take quite a different road, a road the company baron is unlikely to go down. Double-loop learning is now required.

To manage the company baron; to manage the politics of decline and the politics of new growth, additional skills have to be acquired – the skills of influencing people and situations. The new reborn politician must be able to influence by playing the politics of management, managing equally well those who share and do not share his vision of the future.

Even when changes have been introduced, politics will not cease. Collaboration will not mean compliance. People of similar standing and skills will negotiate and work together only if there is something in it for them. If you think that politics are complex now, they will be even more so in the future.

Part Three
THE POLITICS
OF MANAGEMENT

In conversation

Plant manager (drunk, still drinking and generally depressed): It was that bastard Frederikson. This place is like it is because of that arse 'ole!

Junior executive: Didn't really know him that well, Mr Dawson.

Plant manager (shouting): You're dead right you didn't. You're dead right you didn't!

Junior executive: But I thought he got the KY contract and then those three other contracts with the Norsca Group. Saved this division didn't .....?

Plant manager (shouting even more): Whose damn side are you on eh .....EH?

Moral

History judges what you did.

Your contemporaries can only see how you do it.

6 The Politics of Interpersonal Influence

Politics is a process, that of influencing individuals and groups of people to your point of view. You may wish others to accept your ideas, do what you want them to or simply get them to re-examine what they are doing so that they can improve their performance. Being in a position of formal authority is not sufficient. All too often an unacceptable boss finds that he is blocked, out-manoeuvred or even out-talked by smarter subordinates. What is required is to influence others sufficiently to accept your particular ideas and efforts.

There are seven approaches to effective interpersonal influence:

1 identify the stakeholders;
2 keep the stakeholders comfortable;
3 fit the image;
4 use the network;
5 make deals;
6 withhold and withdraw;
7 if all else fails...

IDENTIFY THE STAKEHOLDERS

The stakeholders are the people who have a commitment to act in particular ways. They have invested time, effort and resources to ensure that their objectives are adopted by the others. The stakeholders are the ones who are likely to influence what should be done and how it should be done. The only way to understand the pressures and strains is to identify the stakeholders. How influential they can be depends on their own skills of interpersonal influence and their determination to pursue

certain issues. It is not important that the stakeholders have
formal role authority, for pursuing particular objectives is a
matter of influence and not command. Further, it may be
difficult to identify the stakeholders. They may take refuge
behind others, especially those with formal role authority.
People who wish to have their view adopted do not necessarily
have to make themselves visible to show their hand.

Mapping the company barons

I was recently assigned to act as consultant to a multinational
organisation at its key office in the Republic of Ireland. The
assignment involved attempting to stimulate the managers in
the personnel department to become more pro-active as agents
of change. Line managers in the organisation needed to develop
greater sensitivity and awareness of market conditions and
become more aggressive to secure further business for the
organisation. My job was to influence the behaviour of the
personnel managers so that they acted not as administrators but as
agents/catalysts of internal change. They could then help line
managers improve their performance.

The director of personnel hired me. He warned me that the
task would not be easy. How right he was!

I began the assignment by talking to a select number of
managers in the personnel department about their work,
ambitions and the role of the department in the future. It quickly
became clear that most of this select sample wanted no change.
They were content to remain as administrators. They seemed to
be more concerned about their job, role, degree of authority and
status differences between themselves, than about the future of
the department.

I concluded that most managers in the personnel department
did not want change. How then to go about introducing it?

It was clear to me that before any meaningful discussion
could take place as to the future role of the department, it was
necessary to attempt to change these managers' attitudes. Their
lethargy had to be broken. Their tendency to maintain the status
quo had to be substituted by a wish to explore and become
effective at stimulating change in other departments in the
organisation. In order to change attitudes, however, I needed to
examine the personality structure, thoughts, feelings and
potential of each individual manager in the personnel
department.

Hence my strategy was, first, to tell the personnel director a
white lie – that his managers were not that bad and what they
lacked was interpersonal skills. Then I organised a series of
three day interpersonal skills training programmes, on which
managers would have to complete numerous personality tests
and leadership/management styles-type questionnaires.

It was then important to convince the personnel director I
knew what I was doing, as he instinctively understood that the
problems with his managers were far deeper than just a lack of
effective interpersonal skills. Having convinced the personnel

director and conducted the programmes, I secretly kept a copy of all the personality and management styles tests.

I took these copies home to sketch out each individual's personality type, managerial styles, preferred approaches to work, qualifications and task skills. I drew out on a large sheet of paper a comprehensive map of the personalities in the personnel department. Then I began to match people together by personality type, work preference and managerial style. I had accurate information as to who were the visionaries, company barons, team coaches and traditionalists.

I told the personnel director that the series of three day courses were a tremendous success. The next step, in order to capitalise on such useful training, would be to initiate a number of small projects whereby people could be given the opportunity to experiment with their newly-found skills. I also indicated that I had been able to pick out the few managers that really would be unsuitable for the new personnel department of the future. I gave him a 'hit-list' of the names and their test scores, recommending that they should be transferred out of the department.

The personnel director agreed, allowing me to set up a few experimental project teams. At the same time, he transferred or made redundant over 70 per cent of the people on the 'hit-list' – these being the people I considered to be the most inflexible company barons and traditionalists.

Having removed the most troublesome managers, I organised a few project teams, whose brief was to examine the problems faced by other departments in the organisation, recommend solutions and if necessary help apply these solutions. Most members of the project teams were visionaries and team coaches, with one or two company barons added in. They had all been carefully matched together from my map of the department. The traditionalists I left well alone. They would simply be ineffective in the project teams.

Two years on, the intervention seems to have worked out well. The personnel department is seen by other departments as providing a useful change agent/catalyst service. In addition, it is still able to provide for the administration needs of the company – most of the traditionalists service that need.

However, the interpersonal skills of the managers in the personnel department still leave a great deal to be desired.

I knew that originally I could not have been open with the personnel director. Had I been totally honest with him, I am convinced he would not have supported me. I would have been seen as taking too many risks. I also knew that I had to put all the company barons on my map.

Hence, I traded the money set aside for skills training for my need for an accurate departmental map. Had I not identified the company baron stakeholders, the intervention would never have made any headway.

KEEP THE STAKEHOLDERS COMFORTABLE

To be effective at interpersonal influence, help the stakeholders to feel comfortable, unless it is absolutely necessary to do otherwise.

Helping an individual to feel comfortable involves concentrating on those behaviours, values, attitudes, drives and ideas that the person in question can accept, tolerate and manage, i.e. their comfort zones. The reason the 'comfort zones' are emphasised is that every person has developed a range of values and behaviours which they find acceptable and wish to put into practice. The range of values and behaviours is their identity.

Hence, people will pay attention to the concerns of others as long as their own are not threatened. Once an interaction with another concentrates on the issues important to only one party, and is threatening to the other party, that interaction is likely to be terminated. And why not? People only communicate when they have sufficient interest in a situation. They are concerned with the final objective, i.e. what is in it for them; and the manner in which the final objective is achieved, i.e. the process. By managing the interactions so that the process feels comfortable to the receiving party, the outcome can satisfy both parties.

The four politicians

Below are offered behavioural benchmarks indicating the behaviours the four types will find comfortable and uncomfortable.

TRADITIONALIST	TEAM COACH
Comfortable with	
Maintenance of superior/subordinate distance	Introduction of new people to the group
Small recognisable group of acquaintances that have developed over time	Helping to develop potential in the group
Being given directions on standards required for tasks	Consensual decision-making patterns
Supervision of wellstructured tasks	Changes of work patterns
Administrative tasks	Small changes in resource allocation and task activities
Routine, established procedures and detail	
Keeping to the status quo	
Uncomfortable with	
Changes of work pattern, boss or organisation structure	People who dramatically threaten the status quo
Confrontation	Large-scale changes that threaten the unity of the group

Too much discussion about ideas and developments for the future	Non-consensual patterns of decision making
Involvement in major decision making	Being personally criticised
Supervising poorly-structured tasks	Arguing for changes of resource allocation Representing the group on key policy matters to other groups
COMPANY BARON	VISIONARY

Comfortable with

Established procedures and rules	Criticism, confrontation and conflict
Lengthy decision making processes	Using personal influencing skills
Working towards change within the existing system	Low affiliation with people
Finding compromises, tradition, procedence and patronage	New, innovative and risky ideas
Manoeuvring for increased personal power	Working in poorly-structured situations
Remaining for long periods within one organisation	Working on large-scale change Controlling people and projects

Uncomfortable with

Acting in isolation	Detail and routine
Criticism and confrontation	Working within role constraints and established procedures
Sharing with others	
People who generate too many innovative ideas	Displays of warmth from others
Putting into practice ideas or policies that are considered new, unpopular or risky	Lengthy decision making processes
Displays of openness and warmth by others	Maintaining group cohesion for its own sake
Dramatic change	Remaining within one job, organisation or well-developed career hierarchy, for too long
People who display little loyalty to tradition	

Working on the 'comfort zones' is synonymous with motivating people and gaining their trust and confidence. The point is that different people require a different approach. Each person should develop some idea as to what other individuals can and cannot accept. Otherwise a sincere attempt to motivate may be interpreted as manipulation by the receiving party.

How to make the company baron feel good

The factory manager (visionary) of one of the larger factories of a major biscuit company had for over three years argued that the company's products were uncompetitive. Some of the products were too expensive but had a long product life cycle. Others were nearing the end of their product life cycle. Unless something was done, the company would be bankrupt within four years. The factory manager offered two solutions: redundancies to reduce over-manning; and a re-examination of their product range to meet forecasted future needs, and, if necessary, be prepared to invest in new technologies. Although certain members of the board were sympathetic to these proposals, the chief executive consistently rejected them.

The factory manager invited two consultants to examine the plant and to speak with the chief executive. The factory manager's analysis of the company seemed accurate. There seemed to be extensive over-manning and outdated capital equipment. The profitability of the company was in question.

On meeting the chief executive, the consultants realised that he was highly role- and status-conscious – the typical company baron. They spoke to the factory manager and advised him to re-plan his influence moves concerning the re-organisation of the company. Their idea was that the factory manager should approach the chief executive and suggest that if the above proposals were accepted, the status of the chief executive within the company and in the industry generally would increase dramatically. He may even be seen as a world leader in the biscuit industry. As a secondary issue, the company would also benefit.

After further discussions, and within the next six months, the chief executive accepted most of the factory manager's proposals.

The new scheme was accepted, based on what the chief executive could tolerate. The factory manager had effectively played the politics of management.

A word of warning: by all means work on the comfort zones of the stakeholders, but there is always the danger that meeting the needs, whims and fancies of others means relegating your needs to second place. In the case above, the factory manager lost ownership of his ideas as the chief executive eventually assumed them for himself. Although the factory manager achieved what he desired, he experienced frustration in that his efforts were not acknowledged.

There is a fine dividing line between working on the comfort zone of the other and ensuring that others recognise and reward your contribution.

FIT THE IMAGE

By working on the comfort zones, it is possible to influence the stakeholders to one's own way of thinking. However, to gain the recognition and acceptance of superiors or individuals considered powerful and influential, it is necessary to work continuously on their comfort zones. As a result, one becomes aligned to the powerful other; one fits his image.

Once one has fitted into the image of the powerful other, then maintaining that image is no simple task. With the traditionalist and team coach, accepting group norms is sufficient to fit the image. With the company baron and the visionary, however, fitting the image for any length of time will be difficult, for lack of sharing is their norm. Rather than become a fallen star, it is important to consider what one requires from the powerful other, how long it would take to get it, and if necessary, whether realigning with another powerful individual may be required.

Working on the comfort zones and fitting the image of an influential person is likely to be effective in the short to medium term. Plan ahead for when the relationship ceases to be fruitful.

USE THE NETWORK

Most people in organisations have a number of identities. First, all employees have a job or role. All job holders are held accountable for certain tasks and responsibilities inherent in their role.

In addition, most individuals belong to certain interest groups which are formed for non-organisational reasons and may attract members from a number of separate organisations. These interest groups are termed networks.

The network is determined by the values and objectives of its members. Like-minded people gather to debate, exchange information and achieve consensus over issues that concern them. Depending on the prevailing issues and the dominant personalities in the network, a network can be a more powerful determinant of the objectives to be pursued and how they are to be acted upon, than the formal organisation.

Consequently, attempting to influence people who belong to networks is as necessary as attempting to influence particular individuals in an organisation. The principle of working on the comfort zones has to be extended to influencing individuals and groups. The key to networking is to identify the dominant core values of the network, and the individuals who are generally seen as upholding them, and influence them by working on their comfort zones.

There are four different types of networks: practitioner networks; privileged power networks; ideological networks; and person-oriented networks.

Practitioner networks

People of similar training and professional interests gather to debate areas of similar professional concern. Whether in education, medicine or management, the practitioners consider themselves to be the true determinants of future professional activities. The employing organisation is seen as providing the basic salaries for the doing of certain professional, but possibly mundane, tasks. In contrast, the network is likely to see itself as providing the true intellectual and professional stimulus for new ideas and innovations. The network may attempt to influence employers and large organisations to reconsider their current practices and possibly change direction for the future. The network may even attempt to dictate to the employing organisation how its professional members should be treated. In essence, the core values of the practitioner network are that it should control the professional development of its members by instituting criteria for professional practice, to which the employing organisation and network member should adhere.

Privileged power networks

These attract people who have one objective in common – personal power. Professor Charles Handy (1978) termed such a network the 'Club Culture'; the meeting place of people who wield substantial influence or wish to be influential. The privileged power network operates by personal contact and introduction. To become a member of such an elitist group, one has to be invited to join. This network depends on friendship ties or old-boy links, and in reality, is the antithesis of appointment by merit and equal opportunity. Despite its self-centred, privileged, patronising identity, the privileged power network depends on personal empathy and warm and friendly relations amongst its members. Whether its members co-operate or fight one another outside, within the network relationships are conducted so as to maintain the network and its privileges.

Ideological networks

These come about because different types of people wish to pursue particular ideals. Pressure groups fall into this category whether they are pursuing environmental, national, political or social ends. Such networks, whose aim is to introduce changes in society, will attract a loose membership in that the only recognisable common element amongst its members is that they pursue particular social objectives. Disagreement as to how the network's objectives should be pursued are not unusual.

People-oriented networks

These are probably the rarest of the four networks. The network exists merely for the sake of its members. Certain religious groups operate under such principles. The organisation development networks in the UK and USA are probably a mixture of practitioners and people-oriented networks. People in the OD networks meet, talk and give up their time to be together as much for whom they are going to meet as for what they are going to say. The influential figures in the network at the time will create the dominant values that are shared amongst its members.

ENTERING THE NETWORKS

Getting yourself known and becoming recognised as someone who has a worthwhile contribution to make, is achieved by entering one or more networks. The individual must be aware of the following processes.

Identify the gatekeepers

The gatekeepers are individuals who are influential in the network, trusted by the network members but spend as much time outside the network as within. Naturally, they meet with others who may wish to join the network or have a contribution to make. The gatekeepers will assess whether the individual is worthy of introduction. If a gatekeeper acts as a sponsor to an individual, then that person will have saved considerable time and effort for he will become acquainted with the senior network members.

Adhering to network norms

Once in the network, it is important to be aware that certain values and norms of behaviour should not be challenged as they are sacred to the network. Whether one's intentions are to sponsor one's own career through the network, or to introduce or even prevent changes in a particular profession or the community at large, one should not introduce too many issues too quickly. Each network has its own way of doing things. To raise too many issues in too short a time could upset the other members. It is as important to fit into the network as it is to do anything new.

MAKE DEALS

Making a deal with other individuals or groups is common practice in most large organisations. Whether resources are limited or not, different individuals or groups may agree to support each other to achieve a common purpose as long as there are benefits for them. It is realistic to expect individuals and groups in the organisation to wish to promote their own goals, which may be at the expense of others. Consequently, coming to some sort of agreement about common policies, or at least not disturbing each other's aims, may be necessary.

The way deals are made is as important as the actual deal itself. Making a deal with a traditionalist or team coach is somewhat different to making a deal with a company baron or visionary. Making deals with traditionalists could be perceived by them as a threatening process. They may feel unable to control the events around them and may not even be able to understand the issues at hand. Consequently, if a deal is to be made with traditionalists or team coaches, it has to be seen more as a gentleman's agreement which is to be kept and honoured.

Making deals with company barons and visionaries is a different matter. Whatever agreements are reached between the parties, they may not be adhered to in the future. The agreements may be willingly broken by either party if this is seen to be to their advantage. More likely, however, is that as circumstances change, so people's needs alter and new agreements need to be negotiated. Time brings about change. People wish to alter previous agreements. If both parties are aware of the new developments, then change can be negotiated openly. If, however, one of the parties is unaware of new developments or finds that change of circumstances is not in his favour, he may then attempt to hold the other party to the agreed arrangement. Even if the other party is willing to stand by the agreed arrangements, it is unlikely he will do so for long. Changes take place and previous arrangements are unlikely to be adhered to, but such developments will be underhand and hidden from the other party.

Whenever deals are struck between two or more parties, it is worth considering the true intentions of the other party and for how long one could realistically expect the arrangement to stand as agreed.

WITHHOLD AND WITHDRAW

It is impossible to satisfy the needs of all parties in any diverse organisation. One way of ensuring that certain groups do not over-react to issues which they recognise as important is to withhold information. By doing this, the manager can achieve whatever objectives he has identified without facing opposition that could destroy his plan. In such circumstances, the manager should be fairly convinced that his plan is valuable, even if others have not, or will not, recognise its worth. However, constantly to withhold information is not recommended, for such behaviour is indicative of a manager who cannot confront certain problems. Continuously withholding information is a means of protecting the manager and not the policy.

Withdrawing from a situation is sometimes necessary. There are times when the presence of a manager in a dispute or negotiations is of no help. To withdraw and allow the different

factions to negotiate their own terms, or for management to
withdraw an unpopular policy and shelve it for the time being,
are common practices. The larger and more diverse an organisation becomes, the more important is the timing of actions. When
to introduce or withdraw plans and information are important
considerations for policy implementation.

WHEN ALL ELSE FAILS

Just because certain strategies to increase one's personal
influence have been practised, these do not guarantee success.
Things do go wrong and situations can get out of hand. What to
do then, when all else fails?

The range of options is limited. The most obvious solution is
to leave the job, situation or organisation. However, suitable
alternative employment may not be easy to find. Job searches
take time. Further, any individual would require a reference
from his previous boss for any potential new employer. If the
interactions between boss and individual have not been successful, then obtaining a worthwhile reference may not be possible.
In fact, it may be more difficult to leave than to stay.

The second alternative is stick it out. Living and working in
an unpleasant environment is, however, not easy. It is both
distasteful and demoralising to continue interacting with others
who do not appreciate one's contribution and who may wish to
prevent one's further growth and development. The only real
advantage in trying to stick it out is that the individual can re-
assess his own values, beliefs and action strategies. Was he
trying to do too much too quickly? Were the underlying issues
that important? Is constant action necessary? Certain
uncomfortable experiences simply have to be lived with and
accommodated. It is possible to use the time to re-examine one's
own purpose and objectives, if for no other reason than that
similar uncomfortable experiences should not re-occur in the
future.

The third alternative, if adopted, is a high-risk strategy. It
involves getting rid of the stakeholder. A superior putting
pressure on one person in the hope that he leaves makes others
uncomfortable. They wonder when it will be their turn. Trust,
respect and work performance is likely to drop sharply.

For a subordinate to try to get rid of his boss is equally
dangerous. The only realistic way is to conspire with the boss's

boss in order to remove the troublesome superior. However, the boss's boss may feel uncomfortable for he is having to relate to a subordinate who is operating outside his role boundary. You may be successful in getting rid of your boss, but there is always the danger that you may be next to go!

DON'T BE AFRAID OF BEING POLITICAL!

Understandably, many people may fear the politics played in their organisation. Equally, many people may not wish to play politics. Whatever each individual decides, at least he should not be afraid of being political. Politics is not all negative and bad.

What is the difference between motivation and manipulation? The answer is the interpretation the receiver puts on attempts to influence him. If he is influenced in a positive and favourable way, the person may consider himself as motivated. If, however, attempts at influence are not well planned or well conducted, the other party may feel himself manipulated. Undoubtedly, most people at work will experience situations where stress, discomfort and manipulation are a common occurrence. Such situations can be managed and turned into positive experiences.

Politics is nothing more than getting what you want done, preferably with the full permission and approval of the others around you.

7 The Politics of Planned Change

Change is big business. The problem is to do it well.

Change is nothing new to any organised society. From ancient times, individuals, groups and nations have had to cope with numerous changes. Changes of political, military and social leaders; changes of national and of local politics; changes of geographic boundaries; changes of the way of life brought about by the application of new technologies leading to changes in the structure of communities. Change has always been big business.

Yet, people are wary of change. It involves disruption. For so many people the possibility of change generates images that seem fearful, anxiety-provoking, awe-inspiring and many of us are left with the doubt – will I be able to cope? It is no coincidence that both individuals and the media report the negative experiences of change.

Part of the problem is recognising that changes need to take place. Then people have to come to terms with the fact that the changes they have to work on may not be the ones they had expected. Further, people may lack the confidence to implement change or they may even be unsure what steps to take to introduce it. Fears and anxieties about the future are as much a reflection of people's inadequate preparation for change as fears for change itself.

For those who wish to stimulate change and at the same time be more in control of the process, seven steps to effective planned change can be listed:

step 1 Map the issues
step 2 Just one problem to start with
step 3 Use consultants

STEP 1 MAP THE ISSUES

To appreciate the issues that dominate people's attention, it is necessary to talk to individuals and groups in informal, comfortable, relaxed surroundings. In this way, sufficient trust and rapport between different individuals and groups can be generated for people to want to talk to each other about matters that are important to them. Further, people can explore concerns without having to take a particular stand. When people face problems at work, they often feel pressurised to take a definite view even when they do not fully understand the broader issues. Mapping out problems in a non-stressful environment helps people fully to appreciate their work pressure.

The mapping process can be conducted by holding confidential one-to-one meetings; informal small group meetings; lunches and brain-storming sessions. Each approach could be effective depending on the objectives being pursued.

STEP 2 JUST ONE PROBLEM TO START WITH

Map out all you want, but at least test your ideas just once before putting the total map into action. Mapping is a theoretical process. Until application, it is impossible to state accurately that the most relevant data has been gathered, that people's reactions to change have been well understood or even that the changes proposed are what the populace want or will tolerate.

Further, to put a complete map into action could easily alienate those at the receiving end. A workable rule of thumb is that people are not fond of change until they recognise the advantages for them. To introduce too much too quickly is to overwhelm; to overwhelm is to blind all to the advantages they can gain.

The cardinal rule is – just one problem to start with! If the problem is successfully managed, success will lead to success. Others will wish to experience the one successful but experimental venture.

If success does not come, all is not lost. An unsuccessful experiment will provide valuable data for the map. The change agents may lose some credibility and be required to slow down temporarily, but they will still be able to continue with their long-term plans. The worst possible procedure is to introduce too much too quickly, invest highly, allow the situation to deteriorate and hence stimulate a climate of anti-change that will allow no developments to take place. The first steps to implementing change will strongly influence people's opinions on change for years ahead.

Ain't the corn high, ma?

The keynote speaker at the 'What's Happening in Management Development Conference' 1980, held at Cranfield School of Management, was Professor Gordon Lippitt of George Washington University, USA – a world-renowned behavioural scientist; and a well-known humourist.

To the conference delegates, Lippitt related the story of an elderly, conservative mid-west US farmer who was searching for another farm to buy. One day, the farmer and his wife were exploring an area which attracted the farmer but not his wife. During the car journey, the wife complained that she did not like the style of housing in the area, she was not attracted to the people, there were too many telegraph poles and far too many electricity pylons. The farmer listened and commented little. He thought to himself, what is the one thing I can do to change this woman's mind? Suddenly, he stopped the car, ran out, taking his wife with him into a field and said, 'You're right, but ain't the corn high, Ma?'

Within a month, they had moved into the farm.

STEP 3   USE CONSULTANTS

A consultant is a person who assists the continued development of the organisation by helping to diagnose problem areas, generate new strategies, implement solutions and review the continuous process of change and development. Consultants are facilitators or catalysts who stimulate others to think about change. A consultant is the additional member to supervisor/subordinate or colleague/colleague relationships; he is the third party to the traditional organisational relationship.

It is misleading however to assume that only consultants act as third party facilitators. In medium– to large-size organisations, where issues of co-ordination are as paramount as issues of control, line managers are increasingly being utilised as third party facilitators. To be effective, the line manager must develop third party skills so that he can act as a consultant to his own colleagues.

In order to become effective at acting as or using consultants, it is necessary to understand the process of consultant interventions, for which a four-phase approach is identified (see Figure 7.1).

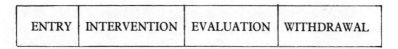

| ENTRY | INTERVENTION | EVALUATION | WITHDRAWAL |

Figure 7.1   The four phases of the consultancy process

Entry

Because of certain changes or problems that have arisen and been perceived, a consultant is called on to the scene. Presumably the client has entered into some sort of search process for the sort of consultant he would require. The problems, needs, symptoms and potential new developments would then be discussed between client and consultant.

The consultant should from the outset attempt to establish rapport and be relatively open with his client. Three questions need to be considered:

1 Are the presented problems the client's actual problems? For example, a company baron may hire a consultant to improve and stabilise current systems and structures. In reality, others in the organisation are attempting to introduce changes to outdated systems of operation. The company baron could be using the consultant to act as a buffer to the more uncomfortable aspects of change.
2 Does the consultant have the skills to work on both the client's presented problems and actual problems?
3 Is it possible for the consultant to build rapport with the client?

Intervention

Once some form of initial understanding between client and consultant has been negotiated, the intervention into the client's organisation has begun. At this stage, a number of separate processes have to be effectively managed for the intervention to be a success.

Diagnosis. The success of any consultant intervention depends on the original diagnosis made by the consultant. This involves 'mapping out' the client's situation in its entirety. Even though the client may have conducted his own mapping process, it is important to the intervention to allow the consultant to conduct his own.

Mapping must take into account two factors: the objectives and achievements of the intervention: and the process by which those objectives are to be achieved. Both factors must interrelate for the intervention to be a success. The consultant has to assess whether the original objectives are possible, bearing in mind the views, values and desires of the various people and groups in the client system. Such a decision cannot be made unless data are accurately gathered. In fact, part of the diagnostic process is not just to gather data for the consultant, but further, to feed back the data gathered to the various client groupings and watch their reactions. Their views will provide further information for the consultant.

Hence, diagnosis involves gathering appropriate information and at the same time developing commitment from the various individuals and groups in the organisation to use the information to stimulate change. In this way, consultant and clients identify new needs and jointly develop strategies for change.

Implementation. The process of diagnosis and implementation overlap substantially. Understandably so, for exploration and application go hand in hand if any intervention is to be effective.

However, once research has been conducted; once experimental designs have been put into practice, that is the time to negotiate for the proposed changes to be implemented.

Re-negotiating your client. Effective research, numerous discussions and appropriate implementation of strategies may bring both the client and consultant to a different point than they had first expected.

Not only may plans and expectations have changed, but also the very need for the client and consultant to work together. From the consultant's point of view, the client he first started with may not be the client with whom he should currently interrelate. Changing clients because conditions have changed is not a simple process. Other considerations have to be taken into account, such as:

1 The original client may have identified himself with the project and the consultants. To cease relating to him may damage his position in the organisation.
2 Other people in the organisation may wish to become involved in the intervention and a conflict may develop amongst people holding vested interests. To show too much sympathy or favour for any one group could be damaging to the consultant.
3 With the development of the project, both original client and consultant may find that they are no longer required.

Training and strategic planning in a shoe company

The training manager of a well-known shoe company hired an academic consultant to run a series of two-day in-company workshops, examining the current problems and future prospects of the company.

Three workshops were organised, attended by selected senior and middle managers. At each workshop, under the consultant's guidance, the problems the company faced were identified and analysed and from this information, strategies for the future were developed.

After each workshop, the consultant wrote a short report on the debate and findings of each workshop for the main board directors. After the board had received the three reports, the chairman requested one further workshop, to be run by the consultant and to be attended by a select number of the most capable managers in the company. However, instead of writing a report, the main board would attend on the afternoon of the second day and listen to a verbal presentation by the participants. The ultimate responsibility for the selection of the participants and the success of the workshop was given to the training manager.

The fourth workshop turned out to be a great success. Conversation and ideas flowed easily amongst the participants. They in turn gave a good account of themselves in front of the chairman and the main board. Some of the ideas they presented were adopted by the board as part of their strategic planning.

The only unfortunate consequence of the final workshop was that it became noticeable to most that the training manager was out of his depth. The training manager was a team coach, good at dealing with people. His intellect however did not stretch to handling strategic development issues.

The consultant quickly realised the inabilities of his client and allied himself to the director of personnel and training. He suggested to the director of personnel that the training manager should no longer be used in the strategic planning of the company's personnel. The director agreed and without any explanation to the training manager, transferred him to a subsidiary of the company. The consultant survived and is now working with the main board.

Evaluation

Both client and consultant should evaluate the intervention in
some way. The assessment may take the form of a discussion or
a more controlled study with questionnaires and other types of
survey techniques.

Conducting an evaluation*

For any manager wishing to determine whether a consultancy
intervention has been valuable, four separate, but interdependent
elements have to be considered:

1 Areas of evaluation:
  (a) client/consultant relationship; includes the personal and
     professional relationship between client, client system and
     consultant;
  (b) consulting/training events; includes assessing survey-
     feedback meetings. Assessing the input and contribution of
     these types of events in turn influences the future design of
     the project;
  (c) progress towards specific goals; it is important to generate
     criteria which helps the client understand his progress in
     the project.
2 Criteria for evaluation:
  (a) cost v profit; includes consulting time and expenses v
     outcomes such as increased sales or decreasing costs;
     work pattern changes such as reduced turnover, less
     absenteeism, fewer grievances;
  (b) behaviour observation, such as, is the client more relaxed and
     functioning in a more assertive manner?
  (c) changes in organisation structures, such as simplifying lines
     of communication;
  (d) reactions of the client(s) to the consulting process, such as
     the client's expressed feelings about the consulting relation-
     ship, participant's evaluation of a training event, dominant
     attitudes in the client organisation elicited by attitude
     surveys.
3 Sources of data
  (a) the sponsors, those who have a strong interest in the
     initiation, progress and final outcome of the intervention,
     such as a key manager, board of directors, executive com-
     mittee etc.;
  (b) the client, the person who makes the 'go or no-go' decisions
     about the direction and development of the intervention;
  (c) the client system; any person or group directly involved or
     affected by the intervention;
  (d) the consultant.
4 Methods of data collection:
  (a) observation, such as noting individual and group behaviour
     as it relates to job performance;

---

* See selective bibliography for Chapter 7, page 168.

(b) questionnaires; these are designed and standardised formats that ask for individual written responses concerning attitudes, viewpoints, opinions, perceptions;
(c) interviews; face-to-face or person-to-group, in-depth perceptions, ideas and feelings;
(d) documentation of archival and current records, recorded data which show changes and trends resulting from the intervention;
(e) instruments; specially designed data collection devices whose aim is to stimulate individual feedback about a situation and provide a framework for further evaluation.

Withdrawal

Withdrawal involves bringing the project to an end. It is about how the consultant involves himself less and less with his client. There are three rules to ensure effective withdrawal:

1 It should be a decision acceptable to both consultant and client. Any catalyst should realise that his contribution will, in time, be no longer required. Hence, the consultant's involvement must be reduced. Usually, the decision to reduce involvement is made by one or other party, but it should be acceptable to both.

2 Emphasise the client's position in the organisation. The client took a risk in identifying himself with a new project. The consultant can strengthen his client's credibility in the organisation by emphasising the achievements of the intervention and the client's contribution to the project. By so doing, the continued development of the project is almost certainly assured after the consultant's departure.

3 Ensure that the door is always open for further work with the client. Another reason for focusing on the client and the project in the organisation is that the consultant could be further utilised in the future. If the consultant is seen as having performed effectively in terms of both task expertise and also as having 'fitted in' to the client organisation, he becomes a valuable asset. He has credibility.

STEP 4   HIRE FOR INNOVATION : REWARD FOR LOYALTY

Once the visionaries know where they are going; once they have identified fairly clear strategies; once they are aware of the pitfalls and appreciate how to sub-divide strategies into tactics; the time has come to hire the others to make it all work. Other visionaries are needed for their intuition, insight and flair. The traditionalist is required for his capacity to manage the paper-work and the details. The team coach is required.for his people/motivating skills. On being hired, all will be fed the same story: we are embarking into a new era of the organisation's development; bright, talented, energetic people are required; your particular contribution will be both unique and highly valued; it is not going to be easy, but I pay well those people who get results.

Not quite! That is what you are told when hired. You may be hired for your talents; you are paid for your loyalty.

The greater the degree of change, the more important it becomes to consider values, culture, future organisational identity as well as the application of particular techniques and systems. Through manoeuvre, energy and utter force, the visionary may have his particular view accepted as the strategy to pursue. However, thinking about values and the future is not his prerogative. Most people have thought about such issues at some point in their lives. Sooner or later, the others will question the values under which they operate. Those that accept the values under which they operate will be rewarded, the rest removed.

Clash of the visionaries

A well-known professor of management at a world-famous business school had recently been appointed to develop a new department. He set about the task energetically, winning research contracts with outside organisations to pay for the salaries of the new staff he was hiring in his department. One appointee in particular came from a different background to the others – he had little academic experience.

This man quickly established a reputation as a highly competent business teacher and consultant. Within a year of his appointment, the relationship between himself and the professor deteriorioated. He wished to develop his role as a consultant; the professor stated he wanted more research output for publication. He wished for more time away from the business school on in-company projects; the professor wanted a fair share-out of the tiresome tasks of course tutorships and teaching on standard management pro-grammes – essential bread and butter revenue for the group.

As the relationship between the professor and the new man worsened, so deteriorated the relationship between the appointee and his colleagues. They resented his attitude and his unwillingness to take on the tedious duties no one wanted but all had to do. Within three years, he left.

> This man wished to develop new and innovative activities in one particular field. The professor agreed as long as other duties were not excluded. The professor rightly identified himself with the overall values of the business school and its approaches to work. The new man could not share those values. He wished to establish his own for himself whilst at the business school.

The moral of the story applies to everyone – you cannot be treated fundamentally differently from others, unless you are very, very important.

STEP 5   DEVELOP MANAGEMENT DEVELOPMENT

An effective means of influencing people's behaviour and attitudes is to provide them with appropriate training experiences. Two objectives can be achieved by management development training: improve the skills of people in the use of particular techniques: and change the attitudes, values and general behaviour of people towards their work, their colleagues, superiors, subordinates and towards the total organisation.

There are a number of different training approaches. New developments in computer-assisted learning systems will eventually do away with lecturers, lectures and case studies. Managers in charge of their own training and development are likely to achieve this by sitting in front of a computer terminal in the very near future.

However, the case study approach will be difficult to dislodge for it has stood the test of time. Managers have benefited from examining and analysing specific situations in organisations by reading the relevant case history.

Equally successful have been the multidisciplinary management training programmes of a few weeks' duration. Managers are trained in the basic disciplines of management and given the opportunity on their training programmes to discuss how to use the information they have learnt back at work.

An innovation pioneered by the marketing group at Cranfield School of Management (UK) has been the concept of distance learning. Instead of placing the professional business teacher on a pedestal as the expert, the Cranfield group has developed a sophisticated and flexible set of marketing teaching packages to be used by the in-company trainer to meet his various needs. The marketing group trains the in-company trainer in the many and varied ways of using the distance teaching package. The assumption behind such a concept is that although the marketing group may be experts in marketing, they are not experts in the particular problems the company is facing. The managers in the company are their own experts on their own company. What better way of developing managers than getting them to solve their own problems but from a sound knowledge base?

Equally useful has been the development of the more specialised behavioural training programmes, providing a training opportunity for developing negotiating skills, interviewing skills and communication/presentation-type skills. On such programmes, the use of CCTV (closed circuit television) has played an important role and will continue to do so throughout the 1980s. Managers want to learn how to perform better and the television gives them powerful feedback on their performance.

The real question is, how can these different techniques and approaches be utilised to help solve particular problems in organisations?

Making bankers managers*

A colleague and I were approached by a major international bank, stating that they had a problem with their domestic branch managers. Basically, the branch managers sat in their offices and did not go out searching for business in their local community. Rival banks were more proactive. This particular bank considered it was losing money in its domestic banking division due to the lack of drive and flair on the part of their branch managers. What to do?

We recommended that instead of attempting to implement a standard management and interpersonal skills programme, it should be established what the managers themselves would want. We decided to organise a series of workshops and invite all interested parties – branch managers and more senior managers – to come together and analyse their work situation. It seemed that there were three crucial problems:

1   managing relationships. Branch managers were considered insufficiently skilled at managing individuals customers, business and social groups and staff;
2   adapting to new job requirements. Branch managers had never been trained as managers but as technical banking specialists. Becoming a manager was considered a traumatic experience;
3   managing superiors. Branch managers were considered naive in terms of organisational politics and too subservient

---

* See selective bibliography for Chapter 7, page 168.

towards their superiors. Managing your boss was considered as important as managing your staff.

These findings and appropriate training recommendations were put to the main board. The board accepted all recommendations.

Now the bank is running its own management training programme to suit its own needs. It has also turned out to be a cheaper exercise than using outside consultants.

Developing management development involves knowing how to be sensitive to each organisation's problems and, at the same time, using the standard range of management training techniques to solve those problems.

STEP 6   THE COMPANY BARONS: SIDESTEP OR CRUSH?

Change brings with it opposition to change.

Small changes

If the changes introduced concentrate more on the application of certain new techniques or systems, the opposition may find flaws in the new techniques or just generally disapprove of the new system. Either way, the problem is not too serious. People need time to adjust to new systems and techniques because they require to unlearn some old skills and learn new ones.

Training the necessary personnel in the skills required to make the new system work is an obvious step to overcome opposition. Supervisors, for example, would benefit from workshop-type training concentrating on making them aware of the particular problems individuals face in the transition between forgetting an old skill and developing expertise in a new one.

Probably, those who resist change most are the traditionalists. There is no need to clash with the traditionalist who simply will make no effort to change. Pay more attention to the team coaches who are more susceptible to change. Slowly, the traditionalist will become isolated from the rest of his colleagues, who in turn may resent him for holding them back as his skills are not of the same standard as theirs. The traditionalist will soon conform in response to pressure from his peer group and not from senior management.

Larger changes

Managing more far-reaching changes is a somewhat different experience to just introducing new techniques or systems. Those at the receiving end of change may or may not have to learn new skills, but that is of minor importance, for the basic concern is that life itself is different and that is unwelcome. The degree of opposition to change and the problems that senior management will encounter during the period of transition, depend greatly on the culture of the organisation.

If the organisation was founded, developed and firmly controlled by one energetic entrepreneur, it will face problems on his removal, retirement or death. Pressure will be applied by the 'old hands' in the organisation to keep things as they always have been. Even the successor should not in any way tarnish, threaten or change the image of the founder. The company barons will keep the past alive in the present.

Where there is no one dominant figure, change of top leadership is easier. Senior management will search for a new leader who will satisfy their wishes. Once a leader has been appointed, implementing reform will then become more difficult. If senior management approve of the leader's reforms then policies for change will be acted out but according to each senior manager's distinctive style in his own area of control. However, as most reform is aimed at disrupting vested interests as opposed to embracing them, it is likely that the reforms will push the senior managers into opposition. The company barons will dig in and not give way.

The visionary in a chemical company (Part I)

The managing director of a subsidiary company of a multinational chemical company approached a group of academic consultants stating that his company was to grow rapidly over the next few years but that he did not have the middle managers capable of managing and maintaining that growth. What should he do?

The consultants recommended exploratory discussions with a select number of senior and middle managers. The M.D. approved. After the discussions, the consultants recommended a complete management audit including an organisation climate study, of which again the MD approved. The results of the audit were interesting.

Middle managers were seen to be well qualified, technically competent, with a wide experience of work in other functions and companies but extremely dissatisfied with senior management.

Senior management were seen as moderately well qualified,

authoritarian; suspicious of middle managers' motives and having little faith in their abilities; with many years' experience in their present position. Most senior managers were hardened company barons.

The deputy MD was overworked largely because all communications from senior management to the MD had to go through him and, further, all decisions made by senior management had to have the deputy MD's approval.

The MD was identified as a visionary but isolated. He only knew what his deputy wished him to see. The deputy MD was the chief company baron.

It was quickly realised by the MD and the more progressive senior managers that the company employed all the talent it required. The immediate problem was to motivate and train the more able middle managers so as to promote them to senior management positions. Together with the consultants, the MD adopted the following strategy:

- establish a selection centre to pick out the more able middle managers;
- create the appropriate training programmes on topics such as motivation, leadership and supervisory skills, decision-making skills etc.;
- place the more able middle managers into a temporary senior management position to develop their experience;
- identify the more vulnerable and less powerful senior managers and remove them from their position through early retirement, voluntary redundancy and transfer to another subsidiary company;
- push the deputy MD out of the organisation and into another subsidiary company (he was too powerful to be sacked);
- appoint able middle managers to new or vacant senior management positions.

A year later, the MD himself was promoted to group chairman. He was asked what he learnt from his recent experience of managing planned change. He replied that opposition is inevitable. The secret is to sidestep the stronger but subdue them by crushing the weaker.

STEP 7   TO STAY OR NOT TO STAY : THAT IS THE QUESTION!

For the visionaries who initiate large changes in organisation; for those that support, and further develop the changes, there exist two main considerations: will we successfully apply our ideas and competently manage change? and, will we survive? If change is unsuccessfully managed, there is little chance of survival.

Even if change is successfully seen through, survival is not guaranteed. The majority in the organisation may well recognise why change is being introduced and therefore support the new policies. If the change agents are seen to conduct themselves improperly and disrupt vested interests too quickly, the new policies may stay but the change agents themselves may be changed. Even if change is successfully accomplished, the question remains as to whether the existing champions of change should stay or make way for new blood.

New blood will pursue a policy of consolidation. Change cannot be pursued for ever. People need a period of calm to capitalise on their new investments. For senior executives wishing to develop from strength to strength, when to stay and when to leave are important questions to consider.

The visionary in a chemical company (Part II) V the narrow-minded professor

The MD in the case above (Step 6) was considered by his colleagues on the main board as somewhat dull and unimaginative but competent, hardworking and loyal. Many expressed doubts that he could manage the proposed expansion of the subsidiary company.

Opinions changed when the main board directors witnessed successful growth, the removal of poor senior management, the development of competent middle management and the application of internal job-related training programmes run by consultants at minimal cost. The MD recognised that he had a chance to leave the company with high credibility and be offered a main board directorship. Some of the younger main board members also saw this as an opportunity to remove their current chairman and replace him with the MD knowing that he only had two or three years to retirement. Without too much difficulty the MD became chairman of the group.

In contrast, a business school professor had established over the years a reputation as an original thinker. He published extensively in academic journals. The then director of the business school retired and without much hesitation, the professor in question was offered the vacant position in recognition of his unique contribution to management theory.

The professor rejected the offer, stating that he was too involved with his research to be disturbed by administration. Someone else took the post.

Within a few years, the situation had changed. The recession had hit Britain, research money was difficult to acquire and government and industry were pressurising the universities to deal with the practical rather than the academic.

Currently, the professor has little credibility with his colleagues and managers attending management courses. He is considered a poor teacher, too theoretical, too difficult to understand, develops poor rapport with people and writes about issues that are considered to be of no concern.

The professor above is still confused by the developments around him. Despite the advice and counselling of close colleagues, he has still to learn that change means you go with it or be positive in doing something different.

Tactics and strategies

Introducing changes into organisations is achieved by combining the seven steps outlined in this chapter with the seven interpersonal influence skills detailed in Chapter 6.

Well-conducted change is a highly political process. It involves influencing others to your view, adjusting your position to accommodate, as far as possible, the views of others, so that all progress from one step to the next. The steps to planned change are the strategies, for which one must have a medium- to long-term view of the situation. The interpersonal skills are the tactics, the way to influence people in the immediate situation.

All too often, people only develop skills in either the tactics or the strategies. It is not uncommon to see people with a clear and accurate vision of what should be done in the future but an inability to persuade others to follow. Equally, there are many smooth talkers, who, once promoted to a position of substantial responsibility, find that they cannot cope. After a while, others see beneath the interpersonal skills to find that nothing else is there. By then, it is probably too late.

The successful manager requires skills in both the tactics and strategies. In addition, he needs to be aware of the impact the processes of change have on him. He must be able to put himself beyond the Peter Principle.

8 Beyond the Peter Principle

Somehow, we all too readily accept the Peter Principle. We have come to believe that sooner or later most people will rise to their level of incompetence. The irrepressible Dr Laurence J. Peter (1969) captured a feeling we all share about those who climb hierarchies. The problem is, we are all climbers in one way or another but we do not all have to become one of Peter's casualties.

It is possible to place oneself beyond the Peter Principle by adopting three strategies:

1 know how to influence people effectively;
2 know how to manage change;
3 know how to develop yourself.

The first two strategies have been examined in Chapters 6 and 7. This chapter is concerned with the individual and his personal growth and development.

The development of the individual at work does not just involve learning to do a good job. Most certainly, professional skills are important but in addition are required the skills of flexibility and adaptiveness. Part of becoming more flexible and responsive to change involves understanding the issues and pressures that are likely to influence the direction and pattern of each person's life. There are four main influences: the transition cycle; contracting or career; training for executive effectiveness; and work lives and home lives.

THE TRANSITION CYCLE

All of us go through changes in our lifetime – the first job we get, promotion, marriage, children; and certain negative changes as demotion, redundancy and the death of people close to us. Work conducted by English and American psychologists has shown that in coping with such changes, people tend to exhibit a similar cycle of thoughts, feelings and behaviours. This cycle has come to be known as the transition curve.*

For example, the person experiences a job change. The individual may have left the organisation to go to another; he may have been promoted but with a substantial change of job responsibilities. From a series of studies in the USA and the UK, it has been shown that there are phases that people seem to go through in order to negotiate successfully their transition from one stable state to the next (see Figure 8.1).

Phase 1 : Getting used to the place

A person has just changed his job. He may or may not have left the organisation, but the job content is different. He was good at his last job. That is why he was appointed to this next one. In other words, his effectiveness rating is on the high side.

On entering the new organisation, work effectiveness drops slightly. Everything is so new, unintelligible and over-whelming. The way things are done in the new place is so unfamiliar that the individual is likely to feel that he cannot make plans, cannot make a contribution or even function adequately.

However, within a matter of a few weeks, the person becomes used to the new place. He has found people to talk to and to ask when he requires assistance. If the individual is skilled at handling people, then the other old hands at the new place are more likely to give him a chance. They may make strenuous efforts to ensure that not too complex tasks are handed over to the new boy. People may go out of their way to offer advice and guidance on how to handle particular jobs or even how to handle particular people, especially troublesome superiors.

Within a short time the initial shock and immobilisation have gone. The individual may by now be operating quite effectively. Other people have given him a chance, so he is now showing what he can do. The person is, in fact, utilising the various skills he used in his last job. After all, they worked there – why should they not work here? The person has entered the stage of denial in

---

* See Selective Bibliography for Chapter 8, page 168.

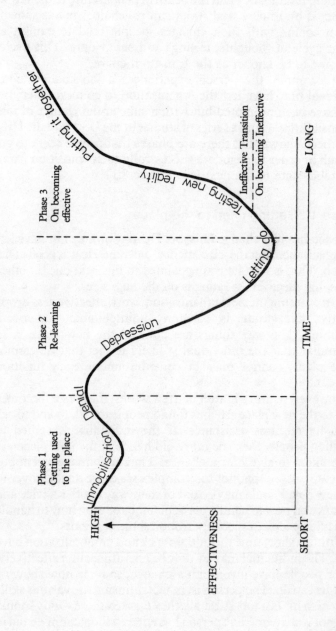

Figure 8.1 Changes of work effectiveness during transition

that no great changes on his part are required. His attitude is: 'OK, so I've got a new job. But I don't have to become a different person!'

Phase 2 : Re-learning

The initial immobilisation and denial stages of Phase 1 give way to Phase 2 when others begin to make real demands on the person.

Denial provided time for a temporary retreat. It allowed the individual to gather strength by using the skills that worked well in the past.

However, within a fairly short time after entering the new job, denial can no longer work, for people cease to treat the individual as a new boy. They want him to become part of the team.

For the individual, the realities of the change and the resulting stresses become obvious. He has to re-learn how to become effective. He may have to learn new job skills. He may have taken on additional responsibilities in the new job which mean acquiring new knowledge which has to be applied to a specified standard.

Most certainly, the individual would have to re-learn how to interact with the new superiors/subordinates/colleagues around him. Departments, units and whole organisations have their own particular identity – their own culture. Hence people and teams will have their own particular and peculiar ways of doing things, and no individual can deviate too far from the accepted norms of behaviour.

The individual will have to learn how to 'play the system' in the new organisation. Being effective at work involves knowing who and what to take note of, as well as competence at task skills. The covert skills of playing the system take time to learn. The problem is that the new boy does not know what questions to ask about it. Most people learn by the unexpected mistakes they make. It is only when problems have arisen, that the individual can understand why the problem occurred and how they could be handled better in the future.

A striking example of someone experiencing a transition is a professional soccer player in full view of crowds of thousands. A highly-skilled, high-priced player is transferred from one club to the next. The higher the price, the higher the expectations of the home team and the home crowd. Almost inevitably the player will be a poor performer for the first few games. The home spectators, the local press and even the manager will ask whether the 'right' choice was made. For the new player, he has to get used to new team mates, a new manager, different styles of play and live with the criticism of unforgiving crowds of spectators in an unforgiving sport. The situation could become so bad that he cannot even apply his natural skills – he may try to run with the ball, steps on it and trips over, listening to jeers and cat calls.

During Phase 2, the individual experiences depression. He can no longer effectively apply his old skills. Naturally he wonders, 'What the hell is wrong with me?'

The depression is the first real step to re-learning. The person is facing the fact that he has to change. He realises his performance is deteriorating dramatically and only he can do something about it. Although frustrated and depressed, the individual can see that he has to let go of the past and face the future.

Phase 3 : what do you become?

What do you become – effective or ineffective? In other words, how well have you negotiated your transition?

After letting go of the past, the person accepts his new reality, his new challenge. He is likely to become more pro-active. He may try out new behaviours, new workstyles, new approaches and apply newly-learnt skills. The testing stage is as frustrating as the depression stage. The individual is bound to make mistakes, become angry with himself and irritable with others. These negative feelings have to be coped with.

From the high energy of the testing phase, the individual attempts to put his new world together. He seeks for new meaning as to how and why things are now different.

The final part of the process is one of internalisation, whereby new behaviours and attitudes are incorporated into what is left of the old attitudes and behaviours. The individual has consolidated his position and is operating at a higher rate of effectiveness than the day when he was first appointed.

However, some people do experience ineffective transitions. They end up operating at their level of incompetence. Some people are appointed to jobs beyond their capacity. Perhaps their depression during Phase 2 became intolerable; they could not pull out. Perhaps they also had to tolerate unforgiving superiors and colleagues who could not ignore the mistakes they made.

The only time the Peter Principle applies is when an individual ineffectively negotiates his transition.

A visionary amongst company barons

The UK training manager of an international oil company was promoted to group vice-president, human resources, head office in New York. The man had fulfilled his ambitions – a Brit at the top of an American company.

When he arrived in New York he was welcomed. After all, he had met most of the head office staff, including the president of the company.

Within the first few days of his arrival, his brief was made clear – make training (especially management training) pay throughout the group, especially in the Middle East.

The new vice-president set about his task with energy and drive. He held meetings with line managers and the training managers of each country, in an attempt to establish what would be appropriate training for each country.

Although the meetings seemed to go well, little was achieved. A more pressing problem was simply getting work done through the group administration in New York. To the new vice-president, the procedures and systems were far too bureaucratic. He wanted to change them. He also did not like the secretary he was given. He fired her and hired a new one. That really upset the girls.

The vice-president continued with his meetings of line managers, training managers and trainers. He now took to visiting the various offices throughout the world. Although the people he met were polite, he felt unwelcome.

Back in New York, friendly relations deteriorated to antagonism. People no longer seemed to talk to the vice-president, human resources. The man himself sensed the change, tried to talk to people about it but seemed to get nowhere. He began to realise he was not doing his job and worried. He was now five months in his new job.

After a while, the president of the company asked to speak to him. The president asked him how he was getting on. The vice-president smiled and stated 'just fine!'

After further conversation, the president hinted that he was not too pleased with the new man's performance. He would like him to become more integrated with the other vice-presidents; become one of the team. The president admired his energy in visiting the various offices throughout the world. Perhaps now he could turn his attention to the problems at head office.

The vice-president felt reluctant to ask for clarification. What problems at head office? He left the meeting puzzled. He decided to talk to each of the vice-presidents about the training problems under their responsibility and what they expected from the vice-president, human resources.

After a period of four to five months of private discussion, a picture began to emerge. The Brit was not as welcome as he thought. He was seen as doing too much, too fast. Others respected his vision but not to the extent that he should put it into practice. In addition, another candidate had been favoured by most other vice-presidents, all of whom, bar one, prided themselves as being company barons. They did not want anybody different in the clan. When the vice-president held discussions with various people, the other vice-presidents felt threatened. Problems would be discovered and the other vice-presidents would get the blame.

There was a serious training problem at the vice-president level. Not only did they need further training in management, but they were generally suspicious of training. The support of the vice-presidents was vital if training and development were to become viable.

In this organisation, the vice-presidents get together to limit the power of the president. The other vice-presidents felt they could not trust the Brit. People were generally alarmed by the way he fired his first secretary. They did not want an outsider coming in here throwing his weight around.

Having digested all this information, the vice-president adopted the following strategy. He decided to hold group discussions, workshops and committee meetings with all the vice-presidents to talk about training needs. He determined to run some experimental training programmes in just one division for all to see how effective training could be; then make training part of the line managers' job, starting with the vice-presidents by improving their leadership and on-the-job counselling skills.

With the co-operation of the other vice-presidents, the vice-president hoped to develop a series of problem-centred training programmes; then to join the other vice-presidents in limiting the influence of the president. To get on with company barons, it is necessary to join them.

The vice-president, human resources, is now three years in his job. I recently spoke to him and he stated he was just now beginning to be effective. Head office politics was something he never expected. Only last week, and for the first time in two-and-a-half years, he had flown out to the Middle East.

From our case studies at Cranfield, we estimate that it takes the average middle manager 18 months to negotiate his transition successfully. It takes a senior executive three to five years (average) to negotiate his transition.

It is easy to see how the Peter Principle has come to be believed.

Successfully negotiating your transition

Knowledge of the transition curve is a help in itself. Nobody can escape the experience of a transition. It could involve job, organisation or career changes. Simply knowing what such changes can imply seems to give people sufficient emotional strength to buffer themselves from the severest dip of the transition curve.

It is worth noting that traditionalists and team coaches are more vulnerable to a transition than are company barons and visionaries, especially if organisation or career changes are being contemplated. The greater the change, the greater the stress and tension the traditionalist and team coach are likely to experience. The values or lifestyles of both are geared to operating in stable situations where few changes are likely. Both need people around them whom they can trust. For the traditionalist in particular, developing such closer relationships takes time and during a transition this is not available. In organisations where large changes are being contemplated, how to handle the traditionalists and team coaches should be seriously considered.

Make friends. It is important to develop positive relationships with people in your new job/occupation/organisation. The new acquaintances will, if nothing else, provide you with inside information; a mix between gossip and a fairly accurate assessment of how things are done in the new place and of whom to take note.

Slowly work your way into the new job. Obviously, anyone new to an organisation or job will want to make an impact. But don't go overboard. Each organisation, department or even unit has its own norms and covert rules of behaviour. It is worth noting and learning those rules before you try to contribute much. Bear in mind that those already in the situation will probably feel anxious about the new person entering the scene. In the first instance, gain their confidence. Once you are well entrenched, do what you like. Remember, the company barons can be easily threatened.

Reject the Peter Principle. Do not consider yourself as having been appointed beyond your abilities. If you are facing problems at work, sit back and analyse why. Then adopt strategies to improve the situation, even if it means leaving the job or organisation.

If superiors, colleagues or subordinates seem to be encountering problems, again analyse why. They may still be in their transition curve and require assistance and understanding. They may be wrongly placed and require guidance to a better suited position.

Above all, be sensitive to your own strengths and weaknesses. Each of the four organisational politicians has strengths that suit only certain circumstances. To be able to reject the Peter Principle involves you in being aware of your strengths and being able to assess whether these could be fully utilised in the new situation.

Only on few occasions does the Peter Principle really apply.

Contracting or career

Professor Denis Pym (1980) of London Business School, wrote a delightful essay outlining how managers professionally mismanage.

Pym indicated that the problems of absenteeism and over-manning on the shop floor apply as much to managers. For Pym, the only way out is to introduce the concept of contracts and not careers.

Consider the basic themes in this book:

- organisations are too large and complex;
- it is difficult to comprehend what is happening in organisations;
- managers end up managing the organisation's traditions and not the required work outputs;
- people have become too dependent on the employing organisation;
- people have become too dependent on the company barons.

So what are the solutions?

1 decentralise;
2 become far more market/community-sensitive;
3 become more matrix/team-oriented – develop more team coaches;
4 become flexible in style;
5 become less dependent on the organisation;
6 attract more visionaries to the organisation;
7 become more political in order to achieve one's objectives.

Both the problems and the solutions beg the question: under what conditions do we hire people in the future? Is it at all possible to offer people a traditional career, providing them with a stable environment to move up the organisation and expect the individual's loyalty to the organisation in return? Or is it more realistic to offer shorter-term-contracts?

The difficulty is that contracts have to be made attractive to people. Offering a short-term contract, with fringe benefits, but with no prospects, is not likely to stimulate a responsible attitude to work or the organisation.

The issue centres on the question of prospects for the future. Perhaps the answer lies in offering *multi-purpose contracts to managers*.

A multi-purpose contract is an extension of the contracting-out concept but allows the individual to work for two or more organisations simultaneously. For example, a marketing manager would be employed by a large organisation for say up to 100 days per year but then apply his expertise with other organisations on a part-time consultancy basis.

Contracting as a concept is not new. People in senior positions in certain financial institutions and industrial organisations operate a short-term contract. In one of the large UK clearing banks, most general managers negotiate yearly contracts. The advantages for the organisation are that the 'clinging-to-office syndrome' is dramatically reduced.* For the individual, the re-negotiated contract system allows for a yearly re-appraisal of the person's work contribution with the proviso that he can negotiate for higher sums if his work performance has been high. Essentially, contracting allows for psychological freedom. Through such a system, the individual develops the skills of negotiation, an ability to assess self-worth and an attitude of independence.

Although contracting is not new, the multi-purpose element is so. When we, at Cranfield, have floated the idea of multi-purpose contracts, certain companies disapproved. The standard response has been: 'If a man holds influential positions with a number of organisations, what happens to confidentiality?' The answer is not much! Confidentiality is not a big problem.

On the contrary, people who have worked with different organisations, in different industries with different occupations are a great asset. Their varied experience can be extremely useful. Their sensitivity and professionalism should be sufficient to prevent disclosure of information.

Adopting a multi-purpose contracting system will be as much

---

* 'Clinging-to-office syndrome' is a phrase coined by Derek Sheane (1978).

a test of the maturity of the individual as of the organisation.
Such a system is open to abuse from both sides unless a trusting
relationship is established throughout the contract.

Change and the company barons – how not to manage employment contracts!

A UK-based international telecommunications company has recently
undergone dramatic and rapid change. A large traditional company
that provided a lifetime's employment for its employees found it had
to alter drastically to survive in a rapidly changing market. Early
retirements, redundancies and new areas of investment were the
policies introduced.

As part of the strategy of change, the contracts offered to
expatriates also changed. Far fewer life-long career employment
contracts were offered and far more short-term contracts.

Although not initially stated to the individual, it became practice
that once the first short-term contract expired, a second short-term
contract would be offered. If the individual read the conditions of the
second contract carefully, he would find himself worse off. Not
unnaturally, most of the contract engineers complained bitterly, but to
no avail. They were told that the company was doing them a favour.
After all, they need not have offered them a second contract.

Some of the more skilled and mature engineers were taken aback
by such behaviour. At first, only a few did not accept the second
contract. Within two years of operating such a system, the company
realised that the more hardworking, skilful, and reliable engineers
were no longer coming forward for a first contract. Only the more
hardened 'wildcats' provided the available pool of labour, even for the
more sizeable, sensitive contracts in the Middle East. Not only were
the wildcats difficult to handle, but the company was losing favour
with the Arabs due to the increasing inefficiency and undisciplined
behaviour of their contract staff.

Currently, the company is trying to improve the terms of its
contracts but with little success. It takes time to live down the
reputation of a charlatan. The company barons had not managed that
change process well!

Training for future executive effectiveness

Management training has by now become a well-established
industry. Numerous organisations invest heavily in the
development of their management staff. The forms of training
are various – structured, short-term programmes at business
schools, exploratory workshops or even physical training
involving sending managers on 'outward bound' expeditions to
develop their leadership and human relations skills.

Undoubtedly, numerous organisations have considered the standard array of training programmes to have been beneficial to the development of their executives, for the business education business has continued to flourish.

What of the future? What should the areas of concern for development and training be in the future?

The marketing department at Cranfield School of Management commissioned a worldwide study to obtain the views of experts and practitioners as to the developmental requirements of the managers of the future.* The principal issues addressed by the study are:

1 What will the manager's working environment consist of in 10–15 years' time?
2 How will the manager's environment vary from one country to the next?
3 What will be the skills required by managers to work in these environments?
4 What will be the education and training needs for managers to develop the skills they require?
5 How can these skills be best conveyed to managers?

The study is currently under way but some of the initial results are interesting. Below are the training needs for the future according to the opinion of a select group of managers and management education experts (Table 8.1).

The most interesting feature to emerge from Table 8.1 is that managers state they need information about developments that will affect the future. Before deciding on appropriate styles of management, people are anxious to understand how developments in society, in terms of technology and national politics, will influence the shape of organisations to come. Once the likely organisational structures of the future emerge then training on appropriate management styles can take place.

Managers also recognise that to behave politically is a skill they need now, but even more in the future. Managing groups of different professional specialists and responding quickly to rapid market and technological changes will require additional on-the-job skills to the traditional motivation and leadership styles being currently propounded.

In addition, education, training and development are

---

* Study conducted by Dr Angela Rushton (1981)

Table 8.1
Training needs of the future
(ranked in order of perceived importance)

Issues	Training content
Micro-electronics in industry and in the office	Brought up to date with new developments; future implications for management structure and style
Politics in organisations	Training on how to behave more politically/effectively in the organisation
National and local politics are increasingly important concerns for managers	Lectures on political thought and philosophy; lectures on current political issues and political parties; how to lobby politicians; national politics and the business environment
Growth and decline of various energy and raw material resources	Information on development of energy and raw materials
Unemployment	Information on likely future unemployment levels; unemployment and its impact on the business world
Risk capital/investment	Information and conjecture on areas of investment for the future
Future managerial style	Importance of participation in management decision making; using personal influencing skills (not role authority) to manage teams; more independent professional teams likely to become more important in the future
Social and work issues	What can individuals expect from his/her working life; security v insecurity; career or constant change; training in how to be flexible; the overriding importance of work
Materialism v quality of life	Importance of consumer goods in a person's life; intrinsic rewards in the job and not extrinsic rewards of extra money, status or goods will be important for future; training in improving the job environment

Education patterns	Teach senior executives that managers will require training inputs throughout their working life; vocational, continuing education should be research based on what managers need
Women in management	Training men and women to work as colleagues/superiors/subordinates; training men and women to utilise women in senior management positions
Managerial competence and leadership	Identify styles required for future and train experientially
Relations with third world	Pick out areas of joint interest between third world and developed world; and areas of expansion in third world and competition with developed world; information on politics and the third world and how that will affect developed countries

recognised as a lifetime's activity. Learning on-the-job or just learning through experience is considered insufficient. Training that both develops the intellect and each individual's capacity for intuition and problem solving is required. Continuing education throughout each individual's working and retirement life is likely to become the norm rather than the exception.

In essence, managers are asking to be trained to become more self-dependent rather than organisation-dependent. The demand is that training should stimulate managers to adopt the values and skills of the visionary and team coach and not those of the company baron and traditionalist.

To paraphrase H.G. Wells, the future becomes more and more of a race between education and catastrophe.

Work lives and home lives

So far we have concentrated on examining the life of work. What of the other side of life? What of the impact of work on home life?

Recently Professors Bartholome and Evans (1979) at the French Business School of INSEAD examined the relationship between the work and home patterns of 532 middle managers. The study indicated that: 79 per cent of the managers held in equally high esteem both their careers and their families; and that managers the world throughout who have this dual career/family orientation, seem to go through three stages of experience in their work life. Each stage denotes the manager's major preoccupation at that particular moment in time:

1 the mid-20s to mid-30s stage is the period of overriding concern for launching a career;
2 the mid-30s to early 40s stage is characterised by a greater attention to private life by trying to improve the quality of home and married life. Many individuals become more interested in leisure pursuits;
3 the 40s to the 50s and 60s is characterised either by an integration of professional and private life or a resignation to a more fragmented style of life. The manager who adopts the more integrated approach is someone who has come to terms with himself. The individual has discovered a sense of wholeness. Work, family and social pursuits have become integrated. The manager who adopts a more fragmented style of life recognises that a sense of warmth and closeness in the family are missing. He placed too much emphasis on career and forgot the other side of his life.

However, it is the 30s to early 40s stage that is likely to be crucial. Two seemingly incompatible pressures will have to be faced by the income earner(s): the need to establish some sort of security in the employment situation where increasing insecurity is likely to be the norm; and the need to pay greater attention to home life. Integrating these two incompatible forces will not be easy. Two strategies are available, however.

First, the family could begin to adjust by understanding that both husband and wife may need to become income earners at various points in their lives instead of depending on one income for the greater span of the life of the family unit.

Second, integrating work pressures and home demands will have to be a far more consciously-prepared strategy on the part of all the family members. Discussions about where the family should go and what they should expect should take place before any great work problems arise. Redundancy, possible lengthy periods of unemployment, moving around with the job, and a perceived need to change task skills and career for one or both income earners are the issues that the family will probably have to confront. Such discussion helps individuals realise what they and the people close to them want to do. Preference should be given to the person and his needs rather than the organisation and its demands. However, if these issues are not consciously addressed, the quality of life of the family is likely to be adversely affected, possibly leading to a more fragmented lifestyle in the 40s–50s stage. The fundamental problem is that when one or both income earners should be becoming established and providing security for the family, they have to face greater potential insecurity than when they first started their families and careers.

It is important that in an effort to be one step ahead of the Peter Principle, considerations of home life should be recognised as an integral part of an individual's career and personal development.

Selective Bibliography

Why the Politics of Management?

1 Professor Lyman Porter (1981) held an international seminar at Cranfield School of Management on the topic of human motivation and political interactions. On that occasion he was accompanied by Professor Richard Hackman of Yale University and Professor Ed Lawlor of the University of California, Los Angeles.

2 Gouldner, A. (1954), *Patterns of Industrial Bureaucracy*, Free Press.

3 Taylor, F.W. (1911), *The Principles and Methods of Scientific Management*, Harper and Row.

Chapter 1

1 A number of behavioural scientists have worked on the concept of mental mapping. The key references to pursue are:-

(a) Goffman, I. (1974), *Frame Analysis. An Essay on the Organisation of Experience*, Penguin.

(b) Bandura, A. (1977), *Learning Theory*, Prentice Hall.

(c) Mischel, W. (1977), 'Self Control and the Self' in Mischel, T. (ed.), *The Self: Psychological and Philosophical Issues*, Rowman and Littlefield.

2 Vickers, Sir Geoffrey (1968), *Value Systems and Social Processes*, Tavistock.

Chapter 3

1 The critics of large organisations have been numerous. Key references to pursue are:

(a) Schumacher, E.F.C. (1974), *Small is Beautiful*, Abacus, London.
(b) Revans, R.W. (1976), *Participation in What?* ACP International Publications.
2 For particular studies that have examined the impact that organisations have on individuals see:

(a) Meltzer, L. and Salter, J. (1962), 'Organisation Structure and the Job Satisfaction of Physiologists', *American Sociological Review*, vol. 27, no 3. pp. 3531-62.
(b) Carpenter, H.H. (1971), 'Formal Organisational Structural Factors and Perceived Job Satisfaction of Classroom Teachers', *Administrative Science Quarterly*, vol. 16, pp. 460-465.
3 For a recent examination of the problems of British Leyland see:

Charlton, R. and Herlihy, F. (1982), 'Organisation Development in BL Cars: Practitioner's Observations and Prognosis' in Kakabadse, A. (ed.), *People and Organisations: The Practitioner's View*, Gower.
4 One of the latest studies examining the management style and personality profile of chief executives is that conducted by:

Margerison, C. (1980) 'How Chief Executives Succeed', *Journal of European and Industrial Training*, monograph, *vol.* 4, no. 5, pp. 1-32.

Chapter 4

1 For further information on worker representation and approaches to industrial relations in the USA see:

Bank, J. (1982), 'Alienation, Participation and the Worker Director' in Kakabadse, A. (ed.), *People and Organisations: The Practitioner's View*, Gower.
2 For a further reference on stress read:

(a) Kahn, R.L., Wolfe, D.M., Quinn, R.P. and Surek, J.D. (1964), *Organisational Stress: Studies in Role Conflict and Ambiguity*, Wiley.
For more recent work read:

(b) Cooper, C.L. and Marshall J. (1978), *Understanding Executive Stress*, Macmillan.

3 For recent work on how people learn to cope with the culture of organisations see:

(a) Cole, D. (1981), *Professional Suicide: A Survival Kit For You and Your Job*, McGraw-Hill.
(b) Argyris, C. and Schon, D.A. (1978), *Organisational Learning: A Theory of Action Perspective*, Addison-Wesley.
(c) Kakabadse, A. (1982), *Culture of the Social Services*, Gower.

Chapter 5

1 For further information on the currrent views of certain futurists, see:

(a) Piatier, A. (1981), 'Innovation, Information and Long-Term Growth, *Futures*, October, pp. 371-382.
(b) Pavitt, K. (1980), 'Technical Innovation and Industrial Development: The Danger of Divergence', *Futures*, February, pp. 35-44.
(c) Lorenz, L. (1982), 'Design: Britain's Missing Link', *Financial Times*, Monday 25 January, p. 12.
(d) Lorenz, C. (1983), 'Design as a Key Commercial Weapon', *Financial Times*, Friday 15 April, page 18.

2 Cooper, C. L. (1983), 'Problem Areas for Future Stress Research: Cancer and Working Women' in *Stress Research', Issues for the Eighties*, ed. C. L. Cooper, John Wiley (Chapter 5).

Chapter 6

1 For further analysis of power see:

(a) Handy, C. (1978), *Gods of Management*, Pan.
(b) Pettigrew, A.M. (1977), 'Strategy Formulation as a Political Process', *International Studies of Management and Organisation*, vol. 7, pp. 78-87.
(c) Schein, V.E. (1977) 'Individual Power and the Political Behaviour in Organisations: An Inadequately Explored

Reality', *Academy of Management Review,* January, pp. 64-72.

Chapter 7

1 Little work has been conducted on how to evaluate consultancy interventions into organisation. A recent study is:

Swartz, D. and Lippitt, G. (1979), 'Evaluating the Consulting Process', in Bell, C.R. and Nadler, L. (eds), *The Client/ Consultant Handbook,* chapter 19, Gulf.

2 The title 'Developing management development' is taken from:

Margerison, C. and Kakabadse, A. (1981), 'Making Bankers Managers', *Management Forum,* vol. 7, no. 3, September, pp. 207-211.

Chapter 8

1 For the Peter Principle read:

Peter, L.J. and Hull, R. (1969), *The Peter Principle,* Pan.

2 Several researchers have worked on the transitions concept. It arose out of the work by Elizabeth Kubler-Ross (1969) on counselling terminally ill patients.

   The concept has been developed further by J. Adams, J. Hayes and B. Hopson (1976) and by C. Parker and R. Lewis (1980) at Cranfield School of Management, examining the transitions cycle of middle and senior managers during and after job and career changes. These three references are:

(a) Kubler-Ross, E. (1969), *On Death and Dying,* Macmillan.
(b) Adams, J., Hayes, J. and Hopson, B. (1976), *Transition Understanding and Managing Personal Change,* Martin Robertson.
(c) Parker, C. and Lewis, R. (1980), 'Moving Up ... How To Handle Transitions To Senior Levels Successfully', Occasional Paper, Cranfield School of Management, Cranfield, Beds.

3 Substantial attention has recently been given to the topic of careers and work and their effect on family life. Three key references to follow are:

(a) Pym, D. (1980), 'Professional Mismanagement. The Gentle Wastage in Employment', *Futures*, April, pp. 142-150.

(b) Sheane, D. (1978), 'Organisation Development in Action', *Journal of European and Industrial Training*, monograph, vol. 2, no. 8, pp. 1-31.

(c) Bartholome, F. and Lee Evans, P.A. (1979), 'Professional Lives Versus Private Lives – Shifting Patterns of Managerial Commitment', *Organisational Dynamics*, Spring, pp. 3-29.

4 One of the most recent studies on identifying the management needs of the future is the study currently being conducted:

Rushton, A.M. (1981), 'The Future of Management Development: A Delphi Study', Working Report, Cranfield School of Management.

Index